Love Letters from Spirit

Your Relationship with
Your Soul, Your Higher Self,
and God

Love Letters from Spirit

Laura Dickenson

HeartLink Press

Copyright © 2021 by HeartLink Press
All rights reserved.

Printed in the United States of America

First Printing: 2021

ISBN: 978-1-7332100-0-3

HeartLink Press
www.LauraDickensonAuthor.com

Contents

Preface	*vii*
Introduction	*1*
Day 1: Your Higher Purpose	7
Day 2: Trusting and Loving Yourself	11
Day 3: God Can Express Through You	15
Day 4: Healing Illusions of Separateness	19
Day 5: You Are Divine and Eternal	23
Day 6: Blending Physical and Spiritual	29
Day 7: Personal Choices	33
Day 8: The Importance of Love	37
Day 9: Creating with Intention and Energy	41
Day 10: Free Will and Personal Responsibility	45
Day 11: Awareness of Oneness	49
Day 12: The Dynamic of Reflection	53
Day 13: You Are a Creator	61
Day 14: Challenges Are Opportunities	65
Day 15: The Oneness of Darkness and Light	69
Day 16: Change and Awakening	77
Day 17: Co-creating Changes	79
Day 18: A Loving Heart	87
Day 19: Becoming a Conscious Co-creator	91
Day 20: The Great Love	97
Day 21: Your Individual Expression	99

Day 22: Karma and Connections	103
Day 23: Feelings and Personal Responsibility	109
Day 24: Your Personal Sovereignty	115
Day 25: Individuation and Return	119
Day 26: The Tapestry of Creation	123
Day 27: Individual Rights and Responsibilities	127
Day 28: Mastery of Sacred Creativity	133
Day 29: Embodiment and Transmission of Divine Energy	139
Day 30: Your Personal Journey	143
Day 31: Your Perfectly Designed Life	149
Day 32: Living in Unity and Service	153
Day 33: Appreciating Your Individuality	157
Day 34: Brotherhood and Transformation	160
Day 35: The Role of Darkness	167
Day 36: The Coming Era	177
Day 37: Receptivity and Responsiveness to Guidance	181
Day 38: Co-creation and the Divine Plan	185
Day 39: The Purpose of Individuation	191
Day 40: The Blessings of Divine Love	201
Day 41: Accepting Responsibility	207
Day 42: Personal and Planetary Transformation	213

Preface

The story of this book's origin began decades ago when I was a young wife and mother. Once my children were in school, I had more time to consider life's big questions. I often found myself puzzling over thoughts like "What is my relationship with God?" "Could God be both all-loving and judgmental?" "What exactly is my soul?" "Is there a higher purpose for my life?" and especially, "How can I know what to believe?"

What I really wanted was an objective and comprehensive overview of spirituality. I didn't know where to find that, but I couldn't stop thinking about it. My religious background was traditional Protestant. I had also taken a college course in world religions, which had broadened my perspective considerably, but left me troubled by my impressions of inconsistencies or exclusiveness in some organized religions. I wanted to understand my personal relationship to the Divine without the boundaries of cultural influences or doctrine.

I had sincere faith in God, but had not discovered answers to my questions about religion and spiritual beliefs that completely satisfied me. Deep within myself, I felt an insistent need to know the Truth. In my frustration, I prayed to understand what is true, even if I had never heard of it before. I determined to take a deeper look.

I have to acknowledge that I had some hesitation about offending God, an unease about straying from teachings I had accepted, and a concern about making a "wrong" choice. I had to give myself permission to go my own way, asking God to stay by my side.

I started to follow my curiosity and to explore beyond those religious traditions I had already been exposed to. I began to pray more often, to meditate, and to read more widely about metaphysics and spirituality. I simply wanted to find a personal path to God that I could fully embrace.

On my journey of discovery, I became curious about channeling, wondering if it was actually possible for ordinary people to receive specific guidance directly from a higher source. My growing interest led me to several teachers and groups. While studying and practicing to develop my intuitive abilities, I also pursued processes of healing my own issues in order to become a clearer channel. I became increasingly receptive to the flow of energy and awareness from beyond our physical dimension. My personal experiences of receiving downloads of Divine energy inspired me to continue.

To support my trust and sense of safety, I decided to always include a prayer for clarity and protection as a channel whenever seeking Divine Guidance or healing.

As I continued to practice, the pathways within my consciousness expanded and I often felt an impulse to write during my meditations. Fortunately, I had been working with educational kinesiology exercises to balance and integrate the functioning of my left and right brain. The right brain is the intuitive side, which I wanted to tap into while still maintaining the left-brain ability to express thoughts in writing. Even though I'm very right-handed, I held a pen in my left hand, which is governed by the right brain, and opened my heart to receive communication.

I just allowed my hand to move across a notebook page. For days it resulted in scribbles. I knew I was not making my hand move, I was allowing it. And my prayers to God were always in place. The writing was a scrawl, but it began to form the word Love over and over for several pages. After a number of sessions scrawling Love Love Love, I received additional words one at a time in a sentence starting with the word Love.

The left-handed writing was necessary for well over a year before I was able to receive the communication and record it using my right hand. To this day, when intending to channel writing, I still warm up by writing two or three pages of the word Love with my non-dominant hand.

By repeatedly opening to my ritual of allowing inspired writing, I received fascinating messages signed by Guides and Friends in Spirit. I was amazed and inspired by the phenomenon of communication between dimensions. I was also intrigued that the messages contained a coherent viewpoint that had practical application. Something inside me relaxed. My questions were at last being answered with explanations that made sense to me and also spoke to my heart. I found validation of the concepts the Guides were teaching me as I started applying them to my own life experiences.

At first, I didn't realize the messages were intended to be shared, but in time it became clear that the information could also be helpful to others. The Guides confirmed that the communications were meant to be compiled into a book. Once the final chapter was on paper, I asked expectantly what we would write next. But instead of beginning a new project, the Guides indicated "Not so fast!" and encouraged me to shift my focus and to practice working and living according to the principles they had explained.

In time, I became aware of the magnitude of healing that is possible in partnership with God and I made a commitment to be in service. Through decades of praying and responding to my Guidance, my opportunities to learn and capacity to serve have increased. The principles in *Love Letters from Spirit* have formed the foundation of my spiritual work involving upliftment of dark beings and unhealed energies to the Light, helping earthbound souls complete their transition after a lifetime, and cooperating with God and Beings of Light in planetary and interdimensional energy healing.

I have been careful to pray for sacred space every time I've worked on this material. The Guides have continued to provide enrichment of the messages and deeper understanding through the years. Now the letters are ready to be shared.

I am so grateful that my questions have been answered and I now have a trusted method of opening to spiritual work and approaching each step in my life. In taking these teachings to heart, I have been blessed with profound experiences and personal peace. I hope the same is true for you as you continue on your own path. God and your Spirit Guides offer you endless support and Divine Love.

>Blessings,
>
>Laura

INTRODUCTION

Love Letters from Spirit is a precious gift from a group of Spirit Guides who are loving, benevolent beings from beyond our physical dimension. These dedicated Guides have made an ongoing commitment to serve God and humanity. This book contains a series of letters *in their voice*. They offer us an overview of the way God has designed our universe to encourage the spiritual development of every soul. The role of Spirit Guides is to relay the blessings of Divine energy and Divine Guidance to each one of us.

These Spirit Guides present a clear explanation of the spiritual principles and dynamics continually operating in our physical reality. They share a mind-expanding perspective that can provide us with valuable insight. The Guides emphasize the importance of staying receptive and responsive to God if we choose to live our most productive lives.

As you contemplate this material, you may notice changes somewhere in your feelings or thinking. I certainly did. I experienced illuminating realizations as the teachings clarified concepts I wanted to understand. I had been in turmoil, wanting to know what was actually true about my relationship with God and my soul. The messages provided explanations and encouragement that I found very helpful. I invite you to consider these enlightening communications I received during meditation in answer to my prayers.

The Spirit Guides describe the relationships that we each have with our soul, our Higher Self, and God. They refer to the soul and the Higher Self as different aspects of our consciousness. I didn't understand this distinction at first; I thought they were the same. The Guides clarified that every soul has emerged from a state of Divine Oneness with God. Our souls are learning and evolving on purposeful journeys of individuation, successive incarnations, and return to Oneness. Our Higher Self is our Divine Self. It has remained in Oneness, continually aware and eternally connected with Divine Love and Truth. Our Higher Self is the purest and highest aspect of our consciousness, the spark of God within each of us.

The Guides explain that our Higher Self dwells in a blissful state of Oneness with all life. We are surrounded and overflowing with Divine Love. Inspired by that Love, our heartfelt desire is to make valuable new contributions to our Oneness. Our Higher Self encourages our soul and personality to learn to co-create with God so that our contributions to Creation can be our very best. Our faithful collaboration with God ensures that our creativity will be in harmony with the Divine Plan.

A sincere dedication to service motivated our Higher Self to extend a portion of our essence into individuation as a soul. A soul temporarily forgets the reality of Divine Oneness and experiences being a separate individual. A soul enters into a series of lifetimes to experience love as well as difficulties. These learning conditions are specifically designed to encourage our human personalities to develop the practices and qualities we need as we become competent and trustworthy co-creators with God.

The stress of experiencing the illusion that we are entirely on our own actually supports the development we need as aspiring co-creators. Personal growth and alignment with God are necessary to work through our human dilemmas. During an incarnation, we are trying to overcome our challenges and heal our unavoidable feelings of separateness at the same time. To accomplish this, we need to develop consistent self-responsibility and cooperation with God. *The very same practices that are essential for healing our discomfort also contribute to our development as effective co-creators. This is the brilliance of God's design.* Our soul's intention is to return to Oneness having successfully accomplished our personal contributions to the evolvement of life.

Our individuation can be a perilous process. The convincing illusion of being separate from God and Oneness can lead to troubling feelings of insecurity and defensiveness in our soul and our human personality. We need wise, loving support to first recognize and then heal our resulting misunderstandings and counterproductive attitudes or behaviors. Our spiritual goals are to form a mutual partnership with God, to create and express from healthy personal wholeness, and to willingly choose service and unity with all life. Our Higher Self is an essential guide in this process of fulfilling our life purpose. Each lifetime is an important part of our chosen mission.

As individuals, our connection with our Higher Consciousness unites us through our heart with the will and wisdom of God. When our developing soul incarnates into the physical world, both our soul and our human personality may be experiencing the illusions of separateness, but our Higher Self remains clearly aware of the eternal Oneness of all life. The Oneness of our Higher Self with God provides us with ready access to Divine Guidance and support for our soul and our humanity. Our Higher Self influences us to seek our own healing and to offer our heart in service to the Divine Plan.

The loving messages in this book emphasize that every one of us is a child of God, no matter what names we use for the Divine or which traditions and practices we rely on to maintain our personal connection. It is important to establish a conscious cooperative relationship with God in order to successfully complete the journey of individuation, contribution, and return to Oneness. We need personal responsibility, an open receptive heart, and dedication to service in order to reach our greatest potential and find lasting inner peace. We are not judged based on how long or where our pilgrimage takes us. God and our Spirit Guides patiently support us on our journey to reach the fulfillment of intentional unity with all life.

The Guides have designed *Love Letters from Spirit* to use as a basis for contemplation by reading one brief chapter a day for six weeks. This is only a suggestion; you can determine the pace that serves you best. It is beneficial to open your heart and make time in your day for receptive communion with God. If you are willing to initiate your personal connection with God and make a request, you can receive Divine healing and creative insight flowing directly to you.

Our explorations as individual souls are divinely guided and held in Love. They lead to our empowerment and to the privilege and wonder of co-creating our personal contributions in collaboration with God. These encouraging messages from my beloved "Book Committee" of Divine Guides describe God's loving acceptance and total inclusiveness. We are eternal and that means we will not run out of time. The Guides assure us that every soul will eventually awaken to renewed awareness of encompassing Divine Love and the deep peace of return to Oneness.

Day 1

Your Higher Purpose

*Love Love Love Love Love Love Love Love
Love Love Love Love Love Love Love Love*

Have you carefully considered the meaning of life? What could be the higher purpose and greatest potential of *your* life?

Now is the perfect time for you to look into your own heart and soul. It is time to recognize your deepest intentions. Why did your soul incarnate into a physical body? Why did you choose to be born at this time in Earth's history and into your personal circumstances?

Contemplate what you have learned in this lifetime and how it has been perfect for your soul's expansion. Become aware of the aspects of yourself that still need your attention. What is the most productive way for you to approach your life? What is the most effective process to accomplish your learning and contribution while you are here in a body?

We are your Spirit Guides. We lovingly offer answers to these important questions from our perspective beyond your physical reality. We encourage you to pray for God's help, allowing insights and solutions to present themselves. Spend some time in stillness and receptivity. Be willing to follow God's way for you, even if your personality has other plans, because this will be the path of your greatest spiritual growth and fulfillment.

After you pray for Divine Guidance in your life, notice the many timely clues and messages that come to you. You may find significance in things people say, in small happenings, or in big events. Certain information or environments may inspire you. Tune in to your own memories, feelings, and intuition. All of these elements have a purpose, which is to get your attention and encourage you on the path of growth that is your soul's mission. You can have confidence as you intentionally access Divine Guidance by praying and paying attention. You will find this method to be quite practical and supportive.

Divine Love and wisdom are constantly available to every member of the family of life. It is for you to decide if you will accept this help. Your answers can be found within your own heart. If you hope to receive your best guidance, learn to seek within instead of outside yourself.

"What about God?" you may ask. Here is the most essential point: God is *within you,* not in some faraway place above you. You have divinity within you, for we are all part of God and God is part of us. Every individual is spiritually connected to every other individual in all of Creation. You share divinity, Love, and Oneness with God and all life everywhere.

The reality of our Oneness is beautiful, yet it remains unclear to many human beings. Your Higher Self always knows the truth of our shared Love and divinity, but you are seeking to become conscious of this connection while living in a physical body. Remembering our Oneness will be easier for people in the future because most of the population of Earth will be acquainted with this concept from childhood. However, during this era in Earth's planetary history, remembering that you are divine and connected with all life requires your focus. It may also involve opening to new patterns of feeling and evaluating.

The pursuit of your spiritual growth and service is the reason you have been born into a body. As a soul, you have chosen to become physical for this sacred purpose. The requirements and limitations of living in a physical body direct your awareness toward the ways you need to progress. Offering your help and love to others along the way will enrich your experience. Actively pursuing your personal development and contribution will lead to your greatest joy in this lifetime and beyond.

Let go of resistance, allowing yourself to be guided by God's plan for you. It can only be actualized with your personal willingness and cooperation. Prayer, intuition, and action are the keys to your success.

God is emanating energies of great Love and higher vibration to all of humanity. Healing is taking place in your bodies, your hearts, your cultures, and your environment. This is blessed and so positive. It is Divine Grace at work.

This message is from your Guides and Friends in other dimensions of existence. We wish to share our Love and support with all people, conveying a sense of urgency for humanity to contribute to the positive changes. Now is the time to awaken and to serve.

You have our Love and solidarity,

Your devoted Spirit Guides

We are all growing together.

Day 2

Trusting and Loving Yourself

Every time you see a deer, an insect, a whale, or any other creature, remember that each one has an important place in Creation. All forms of life are necessary. God intends for all of us to exist in harmony, with each individual expressing their unique qualities. Follow the example of the animal kingdom: trust your instincts. Contribute and enjoy according to your own true nature, allowing the rest of Creation to do the same.

As you become more conscious in your personal approach to life, remember it is best to allow other people to pursue their spiritual learning without judgment from you. Each person's Higher Self can sense what is appropriate for their personal development and will influence the necessary circumstances for their growth. The needed scenarios will evolve naturally if there is no outside interference.

Divine Guidance is available to help you, of course, but each person has the right and responsibility to seek truth and personally interpret the results of their own quest. Your heart is the doorway to guidance from your Higher Self and God. Seek within, trusting that the greatest wisdom for your life comes through your open receptive heart. Develop your intuition. This takes practice, trust, and attunement to the Divine, but it is well within the ability of every being, for it is meant to be. Ask for truth and you will be answered. Your repeated practice of connecting with the Divine is essential for your greatest spiritual growth.

Realize that the Grace of God is tolerance, support, and healing, not forgiveness. God holds loving allowance for all people and circumstances to be just as they are. God *allows* for the events and learning to take place that can lead to each soul's evolvement. Forgiveness would be needed only if a judgment had been made, but God is not judging you or anyone else. God allows all choices and all results because your personal experiences lead to authentic growth. All experience supports you in your eventual free will choice of union with all life.

You can let go of self-judgment and forgive yourself for not feeling perfect. When you remember your perfection, you will have no need to be human.

It is more difficult to learn if you are feeling unworthy, but you can begin now to love and appreciate yourself. Repeatedly giving your best effort with your highest intention leads to self-esteem, even if your projects are not yet successful. Self-love blossoms naturally as you sincerely pursue service to God and the goals of your soul. Respect your soul for your willingness to grow spiritually during this lifetime. Your attitude of receptivity and reverence for the Divine will gracefully lead to respect for yourself and others.

Honor yourself. Learn to treasure your unique beauty, creativity, and wisdom. These qualities are part of you, ready to bloom gloriously if not repressed or pressured into another direction. Value what you have to offer; develop it with perseverance and integrity. Trust yourself. The fact that you enjoy something, finding it fascinating or challenging, is a clue that it might be right for you. Life is meant to be interesting and fulfilling and you are meant to participate.

Love each day for the insight and progress it brings. Love your process of personal expansion and sharing your gifts. Love yourself.

> In constant devotion and support,
> Your Guides and Friends in spirit
> We also love you.

Day 3

God Can Express Through You

Remarkable progress can be yours if you pray for Divine Guidance. Place your trust in God to guide the direction of your life.

Your soul is not limited to fitting every exploration that interests you into a single lifetime. You have all eternity to taste the wonders of life and the varieties of experience that are available; do not neglect your current opportunity. Each incarnation is designed to highlight your personal issues and provide a sequence of opportunities to help you heal and evolve. Therefore, it is best to focus on now, this moment, this situation, in this life. Stay present and engaged. Discover what is possible to learn, experience, heal, or contribute right now. It will naturally lead to your next challenge or adventure.

Circumstances are arranged to support your progress, but it is up to you to make the most of your personal opportunities. These include listening to your heart, remaining fully present in your interactions, and expressing your talents. This approach to life can be very rewarding. Following your own path will bring you challenge, purpose, and fulfillment.

You may be wondering how you can find your perfect path. Concern yourself with improving your *process* of self-healing, learning, and creative expression, rather than becoming attached to a specific outcome. Setting goals is productive, but it is important to remain flexible in order to respond to synchronicities and to your Divine Guidance. Your life path may have many twists and turns, so the eventual destination could turn out to be quite unexpected. Enjoy your journey as it unfolds, trusting God to light the way.

Pay attention to the next step in front of you, remembering to celebrate your Oneness with Creation and other beings as you go along. Your sense of connection will nourish joy within your heart as your soul continues to grow. You are never alone. You have support available, both seen and unseen. Those of us in spirit find that it increases our own joy and fulfillment to share Love and communication as we all grow together.

Play and laugh, sing and dance, interact with love, creativity, and kindness. This is how God goes about expressing in the world, for God exists in each one of us. Life becomes fulfilling when we consciously allow divinity to flow through us. Deep inside ourselves, we all want to create a sense of harmony and connection with each other and with the entire family of life.

Cooperation will lead to creative problem solving and a genuine feeling of community in your world. Creative energies begin within individuals, but they reach their greatest potential when individuals work together in a spirit of collaboration and mutual accomplishment.

How exquisite! It makes us want to applaud and cheer at the thought. Planet Earth is entering a new phase of development that will be wonderful beyond what most of humanity can now imagine. The time is coming when there will be a spirit of peace, Divine Love, and service in the hearts of all people here.

This progress is blessed and it will be joyful. It is destined to come about; the transition has already begun. Notice this and delight in the awareness that you play a part in it.

This message is for all souls, in bodies and in spirit. Every single soul is important in the sacred process of striving for unity and full remembrance of our Oneness. Our deep connection with all of Creation already exists beyond our illusions of separateness.

Bless you, dear one. You are greatly loved.
Your Guides and Friends
We are here in service, too.

DAY 4

Healing Illusions of Separateness

Love is the answer to the yearning in your heart. Divine Love offers support as you demonstrate respect and presence with your companions. Loving connections bring healing to your sense of separateness.

Genuine Love does not seek to control or manipulate. Love is accepting; Love allows for all to be just as they are. Love remains open to personal trust and intimacy. Love is not prideful. Love gives freely, without expectation. Love does not require reciprocation or acknowledgment, for Love is its own reward. Love brings peace.

God lovingly accepts your process of growth and appreciates your progress, whether it involves contentment or turmoil. Your devotion to God is meant to include Love for yourself as well as Love for others. When you respect yourself, it is easier to generously extend respect to those around you. Unconditional Love fosters inner peace and builds community and connection.

For Divine Love to be deeply felt, it must be allowed in. Create rituals and occasions in your life to intentionally open your heart to Love. Willingly accept the power and Grace of God. You will find that allowing Divine Love to fill your heart is a process of openness and receptivity rather than effort.

God's Love for you is constant. We love and support you, too. There is also love and assistance available for you from your physical companions, if you remain receptive.

The universe contributes to your soul's evolvement by reflecting to you the assumptions you make. Your experiences and emotional reactions highlight your assumptions, giving you the opportunity to notice each one and to reevaluate them as needed.

Individuals often maintain illusions that they are different from other people or separate from certain advantages or misfortunes in life. Some people may feel more deserving or less deserving than others. Some may feel that they are more in control or less in control than others.

Your birth into the physical world is like your soul enrolling in a school. Experiencing individuality is part of the curriculum you have agreed to. An important part of your spiritual growth on Earth is to identify and dissolve your counterproductive illusions of separateness while at the same time honoring and developing your sacred potential as an individual.

You may need to accomplish some personal changes

in order to heal the discomfort you encounter here, but as you attain your sense of wholeness and purpose you will feel very rewarded. The function of your unease is to nudge you toward the progress your soul is seeking. This is the reason discomfort is an important part of your soul's journey. The personal shifts and new habits you need to develop in order to feel better are what will enable you to become an effective co-creator with God. Co-creation is your bigger goal.

As you acknowledge any aspects of your ego that are out of integrity or stubbornly persisting in a painful experience of separateness, you can regard them with compassion rather than judgment. They need to be healed, rather than hidden or pushed away.

With God's help, your feelings of separateness and insecurity can be gathered in and returned to Love. As you heal, you develop personal wholeness and a sense of confidence. You begin to feel the profound awareness of Oneness with all Creation that is your right and your deepest need.

Mankind has free will. You can welcome your process of spiritual growth by remaining aware, asking for God's help, and persevering, or you can resist it by denial, procrastination, or rebellion. It is completely your choice. Either choice will be accepted, but one path brings you peace and the other brings difficulty. Dissatisfaction with the results of your choices may provide you with needed motivation for change. Your

Higher Self will continue arranging opportunities for you to willingly embrace your personal growth.

Remember you are deeply loved. Divine Love flows among all beings and connects us like a shimmering web. The beautiful and uplifting awareness of Love is available to each of us through our attitudes of reverence and loving allowance.

Let go of judgment toward yourself and others. Open your heart with empathy and compassion. Realize that everything is evolving with a purpose. Accepting your experiences and recognizing your true feelings can guide you toward reaching your personal wholeness. Everything in your reality is structured to encourage your process of healing and development.

God's universe is perfect in its design. Each individual has a spark of divine perfection as well. Trust your process of evolving. You can contribute and serve while you are healing your sense of separation and honoring your Oneness with God.

Bless you, dear friend. We are always nearby. You are never alone. We honor you and applaud your continuing growth.

> You are a precious member of our family.
>
> Your Guides and Friends in spirit
>
> You are loved. Love yourself and love all others.

DAY 5

You Are Divine and Eternal

Divine Love is always ready to respond to you. See yourself as part of all life and see all life as part of you. We are all connected and can be coordinated with each other through God. Constructively interacting with others as God guides us will ultimately create Heaven on Earth.

We are all part of the totality of God. The Presence of God dwells within each individual. You will feel complete when you fully realize your Oneness with all others and your Source. The peace that accompanies this awakening is profound and uplifting. It is so encouraging to notice the awareness of Oneness emerging in your world. The Truth is being shared throughout your global civilization by many unique voices. Mankind will heal as everyone's inherent divinity is recognized and honored. God has planned and blessed this worldwide healing. It is coming about, for it is needed and destined.

Earthquakes, floods, and hurricanes may seem to be terrible disasters, but all things that occur are needed in some way by the souls that are impacted. From the perspective of the Higher Self, no one is a victim of circumstances or tragedies. All events are potentially positive depending on the personality's response. Nothing happens to anyone that is not for their soul's greatest growth. Each person's Higher Self influences the conditions their personality faces, but this takes place beyond the individual's conscious awareness. God provides guidance toward solutions or peace of mind when a person seeks Divine help.

Misfortunes are actually opportunities for growth created with the full permission of each individual's Higher Consciousness. Difficult situations often provide surprising new avenues to God and community. There may be bonding through caring for each other or facing a crisis together. Compassion for others, grief, or even despair may lead to an essential opening of a person's heart. Certain stressful circumstances may also be opportunities for accomplishing specific personal development or for choosing different priorities. Personal qualities or abilities that an individual strengthens by meeting challenges often become essential to that person's growth or mission of service.

Remember, you are eternal. Your soul still has learning to accomplish and will have many lifetimes and bodies with a great variety of experiences. Even someone's death may provide a valuable spiritual lesson for their soul's progress. From the long-range perspective of your Higher Self, *all* learning is progress through the illusions of separation and is therefore positive.

Be optimistic. You have the potential to succeed in every lifetime. By success we refer to your soul's evolvement and contribution, not to health, status, or material wealth. Following your soul's best path nourishes your character development and fulfillment in this lifetime and beyond.

Growth is more difficult if you are feeling tense or fearful, so do your best to let go of any resistance to the learning immediately in front of you. Relax and trust in the perfection of the planning and guidance that God and your Higher Self provide for your life. As an autonomous soul, you always have free will and choice. You can take responsibility for your own experience of reality by how you choose to view that reality and how you choose to respond.

Will you react with tension, tantrums, or attempts to control, or will you open your heart and gratefully allow your life path to be guided by God? Will you yield to the wisdom that carefully guides you from within?

Take time to be still and attune to your Divine Guidance, the soft voice inside you. It can be your greatest strength and inspiration. For positive results, maintain your personal spiritual practice. Frequently connecting with God is the way you are designed to function best. Learn to work with the process of seeking and receiving inner guidance. Resistance can lead to delays of stagnation or counterproductive directions. This is also valuable learning, but somewhat of a detour.

You are given many chances to progress on your soul's chosen path. You have the sovereign right to make your own choices and to learn by experiencing the results of those choices. Your personal life experiences provide opportunities for meaningful, authentic growth.

You came from God. You are engaged in a process of discovering Divine wisdom deep within yourself and learning to love and trust it. As your Spirit Guides, we support all the choices you make in your process of self-discovery, the more efficient choices that produce immediate healing, fulfillment, or joy, as well as the less efficient choices. The consequences and insights from your less efficient choices can still lead you to wonderful results, but through a less direct process.

You are continually evolving. All pleasant and unpleasant lessons can be positive because they create opportunities for growth. You are eternal; you have plenty of time to develop and express yourself. The urgency right now is for individuals and awakened humanity as a whole to ease the deep suffering that persists on Earth. It is time to heal the sense of separateness and mistaken assumptions that have resulted in widespread distortion and pain in your world. Your dedication and cooperation with God are essential as you heal conditions on your planet.

You are always safe, for God loves you and will never abandon you. Even when your body dies, you are alive, conscious, and safe. Be patient and respectful with yourself, remembering that you are divine. Your innermost being is exquisite and radiant. Trust yourself when you are intentionally aligning with God and your sacred Higher Self.

Life is meant to be purposeful and challenging, but not overwhelming. Earth experience is meant to be a wonderful time of accelerated growth, accomplishment, and experiencing love. In time, life on Earth is destined to become loving and spiritually productive for all souls who dwell here.

> May peace be in your heart.
>
> Your Spirit Guides and Friends
>
> Divine Love and compassion are here for you right now.

DAY 6

BLENDING PHYSICAL AND SPIRITUAL

You are both spiritual and physical during an incarnation, so it is important that you sustain both aspects of your being. If you choose to make the most of your lifetime, neither aspect should be allowed to crowd out the other. Nourish your heart by finding your own balance of devotion to God and service to others.

Allow the things you love to remain in your life. There are activities that nurture your soul, gatherings or environments that elevate you, and objects that bring you comfort or inspiration. It is beneficial to appreciate those things in the physical world that also serve you spiritually.

In times of quiet contemplation, notice which people and environments feel genuinely supportive. Connect with them, knowing that balance is important for your emotional health. These connections can help you cope with the more challenging and stressful situations that occur in your life. Taking time to nourish your inner self is not a luxury; it is essential for your stability and well-being.

You were born to be involved with your life experiences. You are learning to stay present with people, situations and opportunities. This grounding is valuable. Do not consider it time away from more spiritual pursuits, for it is an important part of your spiritual growth. Your involvement leads to recognizing Oneness. Involvement, contemplation, and replenishment are all beneficial for your human personality.

You are in the process of developing your authentic self and evolving toward your most positive personal expression. This is your service to God and to your own soul. Realizing that God dwells within you may be a new perspective for many people, but this understanding leads to your greatest growth. Human beings are learning to access their inner divinity in order to create true community and remarkable improvements in your world. This progress is a glorious goal, well worth an adjustment in thinking.

You can ask for the help you need as you are living and learning. Your meaningful growth process is the reason you have chosen to be here. You are designed to function to your fullest capacity by attuning to your Divine Guidance and applying that wisdom in your interactions with the world around you. Attunement with God can be achieved by practicing stillness with openhearted receptivity. This method is simple, and you will find that it works very well. You have constant loving support available through prayer. Ask for God's help frequently and express your free will clearly.

We bless you and love you always. When you grow, we benefit also. Our engagement with you is heartfelt. Involvement with life is important for all beings in our dimension, as well as for you in the physical dimension. God works through the interaction of many different forms of life in Creation. Trust the inspiration of your Divine Guidance as you practice living and acting in partnership with God.

> Open your heart to listen to God
>
> Your devoted Guides and Friends
>
> We are all connected to God and to each other.

DAY 7

Personal Choices

Your life is designed to be full of possibilities for your soul's progress. However, it is your human personality that makes choices in different life situations. If your personality has not yet learned to seek guidance from within, you may miss or misinterpret important opportunities.

Sometimes you encounter circumstances that present opportunities to say no. Considering whether or not to participate in an activity or endeavor may help you clarify feelings or define principles within yourself. Evaluating an option might even help strengthen your resolve regarding another direction. In other instances, you will clearly feel a desire to participate, or at least a desire to gain the learning or healing you can accomplish through participation. Making these decisions for yourself is your right and responsibility.

Your best guidance comes from within your heart, through your deeper feelings and responses, rather than from others around you. You are your own authority regarding which directions and activities are right for you. Your personality automatically responds to the people and situations you encounter. It serves you well to attune to your subtle internal responses and find the courage to act accordingly.

You cannot always see ahead to know where your actions will lead. You can only respond authentically to your inner wisdom, which guides you each step of the way. Concern yourself with the next step in front of you, staying involved in your experiences and interactions. Notice the quality of your own intention and participation.

Do not postpone enjoying your life or giving your best effort. Your spiritual goal is to have a productive and fulfilling journey. The more you grow, the more you create potential within yourself for further growth. Your goals will be continually expanding along with your potential. The more you attune to your guidance from God, the easier and more satisfying you will find the process of making choices and taking action.

God bless you. Your friends in spirit support you in your decisions and your learning. Your intentions and your process of deciding are just as important as the actual decisions you make. You continue to encounter your personal issues no matter what you decide. Your choices merely affect the circumstances, timing, and intensity of your opportunities for spiritual progress. Even if you deny, avoid, or refuse at first, your Higher Self continues to create opportunities for you. Sooner or later you will gain the healing and understanding you need. Recognize that sooner is easier. The process is divinely designed, and from a higher perspective this system works very well.

We invite you to look back on situations and interactions in your life. Notice how they were actually just right for creating the specific insights, willingness, and development that were beneficial to those involved. There can be a positive outcome even though going through an experience may seem quite difficult at the time. Nothing happens to you or confronts you that you cannot handle with God's help. If you pray, you will receive answers. Attune, trust, and act.

Bless you, dear friend. We are one with you at all times.

> With great Love,
> Your Spirit Guides and Friends
> We cherish you.

DAY 8

THE IMPORTANCE OF LOVE

Love itself is reason enough to be alive. Simply opening your heart to genuine love in any of its many forms is beneficial.

Humanity's quest is to learn about love and to create relationships and societies with love as the basis. This will be an exquisite creation, one that planet Earth will be proud to share.

In many civilizations beyond Earth, behavior is based upon knowledge and acceptance of universal Divine laws. These realms are more orderly and peaceful than Earth, with quite harmonious and loving environments.

But the beautiful planet Earth, with all of its chaos and violence, has something valuable to teach those who choose to be born here. Life on Earth right now offers an opportunity to learn about loving for its own sake. Humanity is exploring love as a *basis* for intention and behavior, rather than expressing love only as a *result* of receiving love or experiencing a loving environment. In your world, you are learning to *hold the vibration of Love, no matter what happens.* You can make love a cause as well as an outcome of your experiences.

God has given mankind the ability to maintain love amid challenging circumstances, and people on Earth will in turn learn to share this capacity with other planetary realities. This beautiful ability to love consistently will be a wonderful contribution to the cosmos when it is accomplished.

Many beings are watching Earth's spiritual evolvement toward unity with great interest and empathy. It is not a small task that humanity has taken on, but the blossoming of your magnificent potential for unconditional love will succeed. God blesses this development, and you as souls have chosen to generate love in your world.

Your rapidly developing planetary transformation is based on love, which takes many forms as people realize their Oneness with each other and with all Creation. Life on Earth can be satisfying and productive for everyone.

Mankind is gaining knowledge of the universal principles and dynamics that have always affected you, even though they have not been widely understood. People are learning to attune to their inner guidance, to trust it, and to act on it. There is increasing personal willingness to embody unconditional love for yourself and all others.

Appreciation of each other develops into recognition of Oneness. This is how the Divine Plan for planet Earth is becoming a reality. Love flourishes first in individual hearts. Then, as people practice more ways of expressing their love for God and each other, brotherhood will become the foundation of your cultures and institutions.

This great task requires the cooperation of a multitude of individuals, each with a unique and essential part to play. Never doubt that your personal efforts are vital to the accomplishment of this monumental enterprise. Your sincere desire to share your love in service to the positive evolvement of planet Earth is an important part of your partnership with God.

Your loving heart is even more valuable to your planet than any specialized talents you may possess. Your constructive and unselfish intentions, just as much as your skills and experience, nourish your projects to successful culmination. Your prayers and openness enable you to receive and share insights, creativity, and healing energy from God, far beyond the capabilities that a personality and a physical body ordinarily possess. Your loving and generous intentions also propel your projects into wider areas of influence.

We are One. The motives and actions of every individual have an effect upon the entire family of life. We will all be successful when all of us are in sincere divine alignment. Every one of us is a part of the same great awakening. Your successful process of growth and contribution involves focus, enthusiasm, and cooperation. You will create greater potential in these areas as well, for you are eternal and your process of evolving never ends. You just get better and better!

We bless you, dear friend. Our constant hope is for every person on planet Earth to adopt a grateful process of living, with love as the basis. As you support each other in your aspirations to realize the Oneness of all Creation, we contribute by relaying Divine energy and Divine Guidance to you.

We love you very much and we will never abandon you. Call on us; it is our joy and fulfillment to respond. God blesses us all.

> From beyond your physical realm,
>
> Your loving Guides and Friends
>
> Love is everything.

DAY 9

CREATING WITH INTENTION AND ENERGY

Love is as necessary to your life as breath. Divine Love surrounds every being, although many are unaware of how close and ever-present it is. You might be surprised at the benevolent Love that is already yours. Pray to consciously connect with this Love; focus on it. Choose Love.

Awareness that Love is surrounding you is only part of what is needed by your personality. You also need to allow Love into your heart, receiving it on an emotional level. Your open heart is essential for feeling the peace of God's Love for you; for this to happen, you need to accept yourself as you are. This is difficult for many people to do right now. Loving yourself requires forgiving yourself for your shortcomings and mistakes. This happens as you make the effort to heal your internal wounds and distortions. Your personal work is a continuing process, but you can begin your healing immediately by inviting the energy of Divine Love into your heart.

Every facet of love is interesting. The vibration of love occurs in a thousand varieties. Sometimes love is shared and returned, sometimes not. Sometimes love may not be appreciated or reciprocated until a later time.

Do not be concerned if your love is not always noticed or returned promptly by the recipient. The energies of love and goodwill toward someone are always received by their inner being. If the intention of the one who offers love or healing is sincere, then the results are always real and beneficial. You can be sure that your prayers are helpful, even if there is no obvious evidence or confirmation.

Have no doubt that love, prayers, and unselfish intentions are very powerful ways that you can create a positive reality for yourself and life around you. Human beings are learning to achieve positive and far-reaching results by extending love and healing through your intention and energy as well as through physical action.

Love, prayers, and goodwill are not confined to one reality. Love can be sent and received by souls who are in different dimensions, whether they are physical or not. Many people have consciously experienced an interdimensional connection of love and support with their departed friends and relatives. The blessings of prayers and loving energy between those in every dimension are real and always received by the souls for whom they are intended.

Your Spirit Guides have constant unconditional love for you, just as God does. We encourage you to invite this love into your consciousness, allowing it to nourish your heart. You are so treasured and appreciated. Please understand that we do not judge you. We respect and applaud your willingness to learn and we honor your courage and perseverance.

We bless you as you pursue the variety of experiences your soul seeks for spiritual expansion. You are already making progress. Appreciate all the elements of your life. Your experiences have fostered the healing and growth that provide the insight you have today.

Of course, this progress has not always been easy. Sometimes you allow conditions to intensify before your personality becomes willing to change or to choose a new path toward your needed spiritual growth. Sooner or later a positive outcome is inevitable, for it is sought by every soul and ordained by God. Eventual reunion with God is your destiny as a soul. The timing, the circumstances, and the occasional detours on your path are the result of the state of your consciousness and your free will choices.

Keep going. You are surrounded by the energies of Divine Love and support for the pathway you choose. Eventually, all paths will lead to sweet reunion with God and all life.

You are safe and you are eternal.
Your loving Guides and Friends in spirit
May God bless you and keep you. Amen.

DAY 10

Free Will and Personal Responsibility

The heart of God holds a profound awareness of universal Oneness. We are all part of a magnificent Divine Oneness; this truth is present within each of us.

It is inspiring to recognize that wisdom, power, and divinity are already within you. These qualities are always available to experience and depend on. You only need to be receptive to their influence.

You are the authority for yourself. There is no power or being outside of yourself with the right to manipulate, control, or dictate your personal choices. You are here to learn to take responsibility for your own experience as you seek the best path for your progress.

Personal autonomy does not have to be chaotic or disconnected. Personal responsibility does not mean that you are alone. God and many Beings of Light constantly love you and support you in your choices, and opportunities are continually provided for your progress. You decide how to respond. You determine what attitudes and actions you choose.

If you could call us to ask what to do when you face a decision, we would not be able to tell you, nor would we wish to. It is your right and your responsibility to decide for yourself. We encourage you to ask for guidance in a way that makes it clear that you understand your personal responsibility for choosing whether to follow that guidance.

God and your Higher Self are always ready to guide you regarding beneficial directions for your growth. Your Spirit Guides assist by relaying the communication. You can ask God, "What is my best choice now?" Then stay receptive as you consider *your* choices. You may feel your Divine Guidance as intuition or deeply held feelings. Pay attention to your internal responses. There may be dreams, visions, physical sensations, or external signs to notice. Establish your divine alignment and remember your personal values and highest intentions as you make your decisions.

You may feel some conflict when your inner feelings do not seem consistent with the beliefs of people around you, yet following a deep knowing in your heart leads to your ultimate fulfillment. Whatever your free will decisions are, you will attain your growth eventually because your Higher Self continues to provide opportunities that are harder to avoid or ignore. It is not *the sooner the better* that applies to the personality's lessons; it is *the sooner the easier*.

Reluctance to trust your internal sense of truth causes emotional pain. Denial postpones improvement. Face yourself and whatever is happening with deep honesty. Pray for clarity regarding the best choice for your next action. Resistance to the situations you find yourself in just makes them seem more difficult. You are not a victim. Consider how you can take personal responsibility and be constructive in difficult situations.

Release intense attachment to the outcome of situations and interactions, letting go of the need for your ego to be in control. Consciously connect with God, request help, then do your best with every action and encounter. This is the process of co-creation. If you consistently rely on God and your wise Higher Self to plan and guide every significant decision, you can relax and feel confident about your progress.

Concern yourself with the step immediately in front of you. Attune to your inner guidance about what to focus on in each moment and what to do next. Trust that the opportunities to learn from the results of your choices are needed, even if you do not yet see how every decision contributes to your life purpose.

Life is like a puzzle. If you focus on one piece of the puzzle at a time, the picture gradually becomes clear. If you expect to know in advance what your unique picture will look like and where all the pieces will fit, then you may feel frustrated as you move through life.

Put your life together, one piece at a time, by focusing on each step and choosing to act with integrity. Do not be concerned with comparisons to the puzzles of others. Know that each person's emerging picture is specific to them.

Develop your habits of co-creation. Become consistent with attunement, receptivity, and responsiveness to God. Thrive on the challenges and accomplishments that can be part of the process. The more you are willing to grow and heal, the more potential you create for this lifetime. You build your character as you hold yourself accountable to your highest values.

We love you. Your life is blessed and guided, and you are a creator, never a victim. Trust God and yourself and remember to appreciate your life as you go along.

> Live in peace.
> Your loyal Guides and Friends
> Love, Love, Love, and more Love!

DAY 11

Awareness of Oneness

We are all children of God. We all come from the same Source of Divine Love and Oneness. Divine Intelligence has designed every dimension, every reality, and every form of life with Love and purpose. This is a marvelous awareness to rely on as a foundation for living.

We are all related because of our common origin in Oneness. We can honor our connection by relating to each other with empathy and respect.

There is an enormous need for humanity to create greater harmony and community in your world. This achievement will demonstrate the awareness of Oneness blossoming in the hearts of mankind. We love you and wish you well in this endeavor.

The consciousness of planet Earth is supporting the creation of true brotherhood among individuals and among nations. We share in this hope and effort and we join in loving community with you and all life. We are all striving for a deeper sense of our Oneness with each other and with God. What a wonderful goal to have in common!

This great work is blessed by God and cannot fail. Every one of us can assist in the birth of the long-awaited New Age on Earth. Honor your individual and cooperative efforts toward the healing of your planet and its inhabitants. The work may seem daily and ordinary at times, but there is no greater purpose to be found. Much of the growth must take place first in the hearts of individuals; the changes in the larger society will then gain momentum.

We respect you and your constructive activities. We know that you can make a contribution to the family of life that is uniquely yours. Every individual has a spark of God and is important to the Divine Plan.

Peace, happiness, and brotherhood await mankind. You are in a period of accelerated transformation and this is cause for celebration by all of Creation. We will all benefit from this epic miracle in your world.

You can create profound changes in your reality by invoking the Presence of God, attuning to your inner guidance, and then taking action. You have free will. Your decisions are yours to make, but we are nearby offering encouragement and help when we are invited. We love you as dearly as you love your children. We have the highest hopes for your lifetime. We can share love, healing energy, and counsel, but you are the active creator of your own progress and happiness.

Ask for the divine help you need. This is important, because spiritual help is always available as you learn and contribute in your world. Loving assistance is ready to support your process of receiving. Allowing Divine Love to come fully into your heart and consciousness enhances your endeavors and your sense of well-being. God loves you and we love you. Our devotion is constant. We feel great fulfillment as we learn and share with you.

For the best results, increase your authentic communication with your Higher Self as well as with life around you. There is great value in prayer, receptivity, and heartfelt sharing.

Trust and love yourself as a great source of wisdom. God speaks to you from within your heart, as well as through circumstances, people, and information. Take time to attune to Divine Guidance and God's Love. They are always here for you; simply ask and open your heart to receive.

Your best guidance comes from deep within yourself, not from others or your assumptions about them. Follow your heart regarding your attitudes and decisions. If you consult God and then act with your most noble intentions, you will make the best choices for yourself and for all concerned.

Willingness is the key, and we are noticing a widespread upsurge of willingness and sincere soul-searching among humanity. This is in harmony with the Divine Plan and a joy for us to behold.

We are all part of God and God is part of us. We are all connected. Rejoice in this awareness, for it is your birthright and your blessing. As you open your heart to awareness of Oneness, we join and support you.

We have such great love and reverence for you. We bless you, dear friend.

> In unity,
>
> Your Spirit Guides and Friends
>
> When offering help to others, choose unity as your goal.

DAY 12

THE DYNAMIC OF REFLECTION

The power of Divine Love enriches your life enormously. Love can influence all your activities, magnifying the efforts of your soul. Seek Divine Love and allow it into your heart. This gift from God is yours in every moment if you wish to receive it.

Divine Love is much more than a passive vibration of heartwarming feelings. It is a strong active energy that can enhance the activities that you choose with your free will. Generous powerful Love emanates from God in answer to your prayers. We happily join with God in sharing the supportive energy of Divine Love with you.

God is always caring for you. Your prayers indicate your personal choice about the expansion of that care. It is essential to frequently request God's help and guidance in your life, because your free will is sacrosanct and must not be interfered with, even by God. You make your own decisions, then the entire universe cooperates to *reflect* to you the nature of the intentions and perceptions you are choosing. You attract benefits or challenges to yourself that are the result of your attitudes and actions. Awareness of the reflection occurring in your life helps you learn to take responsibility for what you are creating.

You are here to learn about the relationship between cause and effect and to understand how your beliefs and choices affect your experience. The process of a cause leading to a result is slowed down in the physical dimension to help you see the separate steps and notice the quality of your own participation. The *sequence* of events can help you understand your influence as a creator. This insight helps you evaluate the condition of your consciousness and your possible needs for personal healing.

When you are in spirit, the effects of your intentions and willingness, as well as the positive or negative vibrations that you project, are instantaneous. You immediately experience a reality that you have influenced by your actions and the condition of your consciousness. However, while you are alive in the physical dimension of sequential time, the results of your actions and reactions seem to develop more slowly. The cause is followed by the effect. The consequences of your actions and attitudes may take a few seconds or many years of chronological Earth time to become apparent, but the sequence is designed to help you see the connection between your role as a creator and the eventual outcome.

If you are not satisfied with the reality you are experiencing now, you can form a sincere desire and willingness to change. The power of Divine Love is always available to you to accelerate your changes. Bring prayer into your personal healing.

Realizing how much you need the power of Love, your Higher Self may help you create a life crisis as a catalyst for your decision to seek the help and Love you need. Learn to appreciate the crises in your life as the loving gifts of possibility that they are. A crisis can be a new chance to learn and grow. It can be an opportunity to invite more love, support, and community into your life.

You can decide to change the nature of your attitudes and actions, or you can resist changing. You can choose to radiate constructive energy. There is a big difference between seeing yourself as the creator or as the victim of your circumstances. You can choose whether to take more responsibility for your life or not. In any case, your choices are accepted and mirrored back to you through interactions and developments in your life. The dynamic of reflection is instructive and loving, if you choose to experience it that way.

You have entered your life in a physical body as you would enter a term in school. As a soul, you have chosen to seek further education; but from your personality's perspective, each test or project that comes along might not seem chosen. Crises that create stress and turmoil might even feel imposed upon you, regardless of your objections and resistance. However, your challenges are an important part of the training you came here for. They do contribute to your spiritual progress.

As you move through the school of life, you will find that your process of growth is more comfortable if you embrace whatever is in front of you each day to learn or accomplish. Daily effort works much better than waiting until you are under pressure or circumstances have become stressful. Procrastination and stubbornness are counterproductive.

Tests and projects are valuable tools; they can actually be sources of satisfaction. Let go of resistance, resentment, and panic. You are ready to meet your challenges with God's help or they would not be happening. Practice approaching the difficulties in your life with willingness and determination.

You have the qualities you need to succeed with the specific goals your soul has for this life. You have countless sources of guidance and support as well. God and your devoted Spirit Guides are always available to help you. One of your most important lessons in the physical plane is to learn to rely on God and your own deep-seated sense of truth in every moment. Can you appreciate how the current challenges in your life support you by offering you the opportunity to develop in a particular area? Becoming aware of the way you respond to your difficulties helps you evaluate your spiritual progress.

Did you notice we said that *you* evaluate your progress? God is not judging you. This is an independent study. As a progressing soul, you decide before you are born what your goals are for each lifetime. You have God's help with this planning process. Your Higher Self, which remains consciously connected with God at all times, influences circumstances and events as you go. As your Guides, we are here to amplify your intuition and relay supportive energy when you seek God's help. We participate only when we have God's permission and guidance.

We encourage and applaud your progress, but we never judge you. The learning and its timing are your choice and your creation. You are the one who experiences the results of your decisions in your own life and consciousness. These results may involve drama and discomfort, or they may lead to accomplishment and contentment. *Your* choices and efforts affect the reality that *you* experience.

Realize that you are not responsible for other people's choices or their experience of reality. You have no right to interfere with anyone's free will because that would interfere with their learning process and their spiritual progress. It is also important not to allow anyone to interfere with the choices and directions that you sense are right for you. You have the responsibility to be true to yourself, maintaining your own integrity. Each individual is a creator, never a victim, whether or not they choose to recognize that fact.

Your Higher Self will continue to provide your personality with new opportunities for spiritual alignment and progress. Your evolving soul needs the cooperation of your personality and physical body to be able to express and contribute according to your higher purpose. Your Higher Self always respects your personality's free will, and the consequences of your decisions and behavior are allowed in your life as an instructive mirror. If your personality can heal the urge to control, learning to seek guidance instead, your partnership with your Higher Self will lead to your greatest service and fulfillment. Each lesson mastered creates further potential for learning and contribution. Your potential is limitless because you are eternal.

You are never alone. We stand by with inexhaustible loving energy and constant concern for you. We encourage you to relate in the same way to others in your life. Be there for those you care about, offering supportive love and your honest perspective when it is requested.

We love you, dear friend. We are always near. Seek within your heart for insight and direction, for that is where the voice of God speaks to each of us. The power of Love surrounds you and is always available.

>Bless you,
>
>Your Guides and Friends
>
>You are infinitely wonderful!

DAY 13

YOU ARE A CREATOR

Love is an amazing energy that completely surrounds you. It is there for you to draw on in every moment. Allow the fullness of Divine Love to enter your heart and bring healing to every part of your body and your life. It is easy to do if you are willing and receptive.

Allow yourself to fully receive the Love from God, from your loyal Guides in spirit, from the Angels and great Masters of Light, from Mother Earth, and from the plants, animals, minerals, and nature spirits. Accept Love from the many star systems and galaxies, from all dimensions, and even from sources beyond your imagination.

All of God's Creation is alive. Together we are destined to share in the magnificent energy of Divine Love surrounding and connecting the entire family of life.

Love is intended for every being and every form of life. It is meant to flow freely to and from everyone. Love is meant to be the basis of your every thought and action. Love is the best framework for understanding your personal value and the perfection of the situations you experience.

Love is the basis of your creativity. You are the creator, never the victim, of the circumstances and relationships in your life. We emphasize this concept to you, not so you will feel guilty if your circumstances seem less than ideal, but to help you appreciate the brilliance and determination that are part of your consciousness. You have attracted specific environments and events that are perfect for working on exactly what you need to strengthen and clarify in this lifetime.

It is essential for you to understand how your own consciousness is the creator of every moment you experience. Your reality provides you with a reflection of the state of your inner being. Your Higher Self chose the circumstances of your lifetime as a priceless learning environment, individually tailored to your needs and aspirations as a progressing soul.

As you begin to understand that your reality is your creation, realize that the reality of any other being is likewise their creation. Anything that happens in your life occurs with the awareness and permission of your Higher Self, whether the experience seems tragic or wondrous, upsetting or comforting, discouraging or inspiring. Every experience is a *loving* gift to yourself in support of your soul's growth because of what you can learn from it. You are seeking realization of Oneness with every other soul, every aspect of consciousness, every energy, and every particle in the universe.

But what if you strenuously object to your circumstances and the experiences you are having? If you create them, can you also create changes in them? Yes, you can. Absolutely.

"How is this done," you may ask, "especially when things often seem to be happening to me?" Remember that external conditions are mirrors of your internal condition. If you want to change your outer reality, you must first direct your attention and effort into changing your *inner* reality. You need to consider your own heart, your thoughts, feelings, attitudes, and intentions.

Understand that positive changes in any aspect of experience, including personal relationships, physical or emotional health, finances, career, and even political or global conditions, depend on love and changes manifesting first in individual hearts and minds. If you wish to create positive changes in your experience of life, work to improve the responsible and unselfish motives in your heart. Strengthen your loving intention to become the best you can be in this incarnation to better serve God and all life.

Seek Divine Guidance and support as you move through your life. Your honest feelings can help you recognize when you need to adopt a new attitude or behavior. Be willing to elevate your personal vibration and create in a new way, from *within*.

As you follow your inspirations and positive intentions with constructive action, it naturally leads to productive shifts. You will notice improvement in your feelings and in the circumstances of your life. God's work is accomplished through the hearts and actions of individuals.

It is important for each person to evaluate the condition of their own heart and to assume their responsibility in the process of creation. The motives and intentions behind your actions are important, because if they are sincere and for the good of all, the ultimate outcome will also be for the good of all. When love is truly the motive and the inner reality, the eventual result will also be love.

Mankind is moving toward commitment to brotherhood among all beings. The sacred journey begins in the heart of each individual. Pray for the personal willingness, wisdom, strength, and Divine Grace that you will surely need on your path. Love surrounds you and we are always near. Free will and creative power are within you, ready to be employed in co-creation with God.

> Rich rewards await us all.
> Your Guides and Friends in spirit
> We bless you and always love you.
> You will succeed!

DAY 14

CHALLENGES ARE OPPORTUNITIES

Love is allowing. Divine Love does not judge. Love does not control, manipulate, or mislead. Divine Love is the energy of Oneness, which can be found even within opposites. *All* situations are part of God.

While you are in a body, you may regard some things as negative when you are unable to see the spiritual purpose behind them. However, all circumstances eventually lead to the positive evolvement of your soul. You tend to resist your difficulties, your emotional pain, and your infirmities, but these stresses all contribute to your learning experience, just as much as friendships, accomplishments, and pleasant surprises do. Your task is to embrace your opportunities for healing and service, no matter what challenges occur in your physical reality. Your most noble goals are to keep your heart open in love and to consciously stay in relationship with God in all situations.

There are no accidents. You are not a victim. Your Higher Self cooperates in planning and facilitating what you need for your life. The process is actually perfect, although you may find this hard to believe. Of course, difficulties do not seem perfect when you are going through them. Some conditions are meant to present challenges, providing you with opportunities for growth.

Sometimes the master plan and coordination of your life become more apparent as you remember past events and circumstances. Looking back may provide insight into how well the elements of your life were designed to help you develop certain qualities, understandings, or relationships. You need your intuition to sense a similar purpose in the challenges you are currently facing. Since you do not have the same clarity looking ahead as you may have reflecting on your past, you can attune and listen to the voice deep within your heart for guidance about your next steps. Trust in God and pray for the insight and optimism you need as you move forward in your life.

Divine assistance is always available. You do not have to meet any challenge alone. You already have the inborn potential for the spiritual progress and contribution you have planned for this incarnation. You are perfectly designed for your life purpose. You have everything you need to heal and develop yourself as you work toward personal wholeness.

Accept your responsibility to seek and follow your inner guidance as you continue your personal journey. Do not suppress or distort your deep sense of what is right for you by trying to please others or conform to their ideas. Some people in your life may not be listening to their inner voices yet. They may be discovering that different choices are more appropriate for themselves. Allow them to pursue their unique paths of growth as you pursue yours.

Accept that there is purpose in the nature and timing of everything. Trust in the wisdom of God's plan and ask for additional understanding if that is what you need. Be patient, for we are all eternal.

Bless you, dear friend. We support and encourage you in all the learning you attempt and in all the choices you make.

> Love to you every single day,
> Your Guides and Friends
> God blesses your life.

DAY 15

The Oneness of Darkness and Light

Love offers help to those in need. Divine Love does not wait for recognition or gratitude. Love does not concern itself with what is currently popular. Love is constant and compassionate. Divine Love is forever, for all time.

The energy of Divine Love transcends the physical dimension. It emanates from God and extends to every point in time and space and to every dimension and reality. You are eternal and you will always be surrounded by the Love of God. Divine Love is always be available for you to call upon when you need help, wisdom, or comfort.

Those of us in other dimensions also love you. The energy of God's Love surrounds and supports all of us. We are praying and learning, just as you are. We are receiving and giving Love, for it is our joy and purpose to do so.

Like you, we are working to expand our contribution and fully realize our Oneness with all life. We join with you in seeking the Light, the Presence of God. You are a continuing inspiration to us. From our perspective, it is apparent that God's plan is unfolding beautifully.

All forms of life need each other. We are connected to each other like a family. We are One. We feel incomplete until we learn to love the beauty within ourselves and realize that we are part of God. Learning to love the divinity and beauty within others helps us recognize that they are also part of God and ourselves.

There is divinity within everything in Creation. This is true of the flowers that bloom and the weeds that intrude, of heroes and saints as well as violent criminals. There is divinity in brilliance and simple-mindedness, health and illness, democracy and tyranny, prosperity and poverty. Divinity is present in all beings, seen and unseen, many beyond your most inventive imagination. *All* are connected. All are part of God.

Goodness is everywhere. God is everywhere. The varieties of experience are infinite, just as we are. You have chosen your experiences because they will lead to your greatest growth over eons of time. Each experience in each lifetime, or between lifetimes, is meant to help you toward full remembrance of your Oneness with God. This is why they are all perfect, even though some happenings are unwanted or seem tragic when they occur.

Sometimes you have great anxiety or objections regarding your difficult experiences. You may even protest or make extreme attempts to control the circumstances of your life. Your humanity is fearful of pain and wishes to avoid it. However, your *reactions* of insecurity, outrage, embarrassment, grief, or repression cause your pain to persist. The pain of an unwelcome event does not have to be ongoing. *Prolonged* physical or emotional pain is an indication that a personal change or healing intervention is needed.

You may have the impression while you are in a body that you are separate from beings and circumstances that seem very different from you. You may even think that your merit, luck, planning, or control have kept you separate, and you like it that way. You also might feel an illusion of separateness because of your own experience of difference, misfortune, or feeling unworthy. These views are the result of misunderstanding and the limited perspective held by your human personality. Your Higher Self does not feel that way at all.

If all human beings realized that other races and nations are part of them; that plants, animals, land, air, and oceans are part of them; that joy and pain, success and failure, entities, extraterrestrials, Angels, and God are all One with them; can you imagine what a different place planet Earth would be?

God, your Higher Self, and many magnificent beings in Creation are hoping for Earth to become the most beautiful and uplifting place to experience life that it can be. And it *will* be, with your prayers and cooperation. The era of co-creation with God is at hand. Welcome it. Learn to bless and embrace all the experiences and opportunities the future will provide. Appreciate the varied beings that are helping Earth evolve to a higher vibration and spiritual perspective.

Your illusions about separateness are dissolving. You are ready for deeper understanding about duality, which is the perceived opposition of good and evil. You are breaking free of limited perspectives and opening your heart to the truth of Oneness within God. A new era lies beyond the illusion of polarity, the illusion that Light and darkness are trying to defeat each other. God has designed Light and darkness as important and complementary aspects of the Divine Plan to encourage our willing progress as souls.

While the Light provides attraction and inspiration, the unpleasant effects of the darkness can influence mankind to become more responsible and to make better choices. The time is near when the perception that Light and darkness are in conflict will no longer be worthwhile. People will have made their most important decision, which is committing to their personal alignment with God.

Many souls are ready and eager to move to a higher level of expression along with planet Earth. You are advancing to a reality where the impression that Light and darkness work in opposition will no longer be the norm. Humanity will still have the influences of Light and darkness, but they will be understood as *cooperating* in support of your willingness and growth. There will be no need to fear or judge darkness, just the need to respond to it with more personal responsibility and closer partnership with God. In the coming New Age, you will be able to respond to events with a deeper understanding of the true purpose and dynamics of Divine Light and darkness.

Welcome the occasions for growth and service that you encounter in your life. Your soul has requested and prepared for them. You have the potential to develop all the strength and capability you will need to meet your challenges in this lifetime. You also have the guidance and support available that can empower you to cope with whatever comes your way. You express your free will when you ask God to support you. Pray for what you need.

Trust and attune to the voice of God that speaks to your heart. Be responsible as you let go of worry and attempts to control. God and your Higher Self are taking care of the planning and arrangements. Your role is to open to Divine Guidance, yield to the Will of God, and give your best effort to the task in front of you. Trust that you are being led to your next appropriate step. When you practice this method consistently, you can fulfill the purpose that inspired your soul to incarnate into the physical dimension.

We applaud you as you release the illusions and agendas of your ego and open to the Divine Plan for your life. When you feel grief, judgment, or resistance regarding any experience, these feelings indicate a need to address your personal healing or the improvement of a situation. When you achieve a feeling of unity with all aspects of Creation, you know peace in your heart.

God loves you and we love you. You are never alone, so there is no need to feel overwhelmed or abandoned. Let go of defensiveness, for God is not judging you. God is supporting your learning process as it reveals to you your Oneness with everything.

You are eternal. Your journey through healing the illusions of separation cannot be fully completed in one lifetime. It would be impossible to accomplish your desired spiritual growth from within the limited viewpoint of a single incarnation. However, there are now unprecedented energies and opportunities for spiritual awareness becoming widely available to humanity. It is possible for many individuals in human bodies to attain the deep serenity of heartfelt union with God in this lifetime. Remember, it is not the sooner the better when it comes to your spiritual progress, just the sooner the easier.

Bless you, dear friend. You are beautiful and holy. It is a pleasure for us to be with your vibration.

In unity,

Guides and Friends from beyond your dimension

Divine Love is with you, now and forever.

DAY 16

CHANGE AND AWAKENING

Divine Love encourages connection with other beings. A loving heart works toward brotherhood among all forms of life. God trusts us all to find our way to unity.

Enjoy increasing your communication with all life and appreciate the divinity that we have in common. We are all moving toward achieving cooperative harmony throughout Creation. Each of us has a job to do, a part to play in this great awakening. That is why each of us has chosen to be who we are at this time in the evolution of the cosmos.

Humanity's spiritual evolvement is at a crossroads right now. Each individual has personal decisions to make regarding their own integrity, their alignment with God, and their focus on constructive contributions. Challenging changes are taking place that are needed to facilitate the spiritual progress of mankind. Many souls have asked for these conditions to support humanity's progress toward conscious cooperation with God. This time of profound change and widespread awakening has been anticipated for centuries. A great deal of work has already been done, but even more is ahead. We are collectively working on healing the various dysfunctions still present in your reality. Events and energies are developing rapidly and beautifully.

Be optimistic and confident about how you will contribute to the global awakening. Pray and attune to your inner guidance; you will sense where to go and what to do next. Follow your heart to discover the pathway that is right for your soul.

You will discover that your life can be an amazing journey. The plan that God has for you is much greater than your personality can imagine. We encourage you to continue welcoming loving guidance from your Higher Self. Stillness and receptivity are your best practices for opening to wisdom and creative inspiration. Prayer leads you to the fulfillment of making your irreplaceable contribution to humanity's progress. As you learn to co-create, we join with you in service and devotion to God.

> We love you and support you always.
>
> Your Guides and Friends in spirit
>
> Attune, trust, create, and share.
> This is God's design.

DAY 17

CO-CREATING CHANGES

Love is God's greatest gift to mankind. It is also humanity's greatest gift to God. Your gifts of love may be offered to other people, animals, plants, planet Earth, and even to loved ones in other dimensions. God receives love through many forms of life, for God dwells within all life. We are part of each other and part of God.

If you wish to love and serve God, love and serve the beings, the civilization, and the environment around you. When you strive to safeguard and improve these in a loving way, you demonstrate your reverence for God and your growing awareness of the Oneness of all life.

Remember that your process is as important as your goal. Your unselfish intentions and your consideration for others have a powerful effect on your reality, just as your choices and actions do. When you have an admirable goal, it is important to use ethical means to reach that goal because the result is always affected by your motives and your methods. This principle is true whether or not you realize it at the time you take an action.

Both your intentions and actions impact the entire universe in the same way a drop of liquid affects the whole ocean. There is no way a drop can remain isolated. It quickly becomes one with all the other drops, each affecting the quality of existence for the others.

Search your heart to determine the quality of your participation. The choice to avoid involvement is impossible because you are already part of All That Is. Your choice is between contributing to the difficulties or contributing to the improvements.

If you are not satisfied with the contribution that you are making right now, what can you do? First, acknowledge your desire to change. With uncompromising honesty, look at what is not in right order. Even if you do not have the willingness to take any action toward change yet, the sincere desire for change is an important beginning.

To initiate your process of change, pray for the help you need. Whether your prayer is silent, written, or spoken, it is a very important step. There is abundant Love and support available at all times from God and the many glorious beings around you. Open your heart to receive their Love and to recognize the Love that is already embodied in you.

No one in Creation has the right to interfere with another's free will. God and the many dedicated beings that serve the Will of God would not consider interfering with you. Therefore, it is essential for you to make your choice known through prayer, and often a statement to another person, that you are requesting help with the changes you wish to make.

Ask God for clarity if you are in turmoil about your feelings or confused regarding your beliefs. Pray to know the truth. If you are feeling upset about something that has happened, request help with healing your emotional reaction to the experience. Pray for help to realize that each person involved in any situation has taken part with the full consent of their Higher Self, even if their personality is objecting or unaware. Each person's participation includes the potential for their soul's progress. Seek to understand the divine perspective regarding your specific experiences. Invite the power of God's Love into your heart to bring you the peace, comfort, and clarity that you seek. Loving support is constantly available, if you simply ask.

Please understand that you deserve Divine Love and help in your life. Have no doubt that you are worthy. Feel secure knowing that God has always loved you and always will, no matter what you have done or have not done. God looks forward to the time when unity is freely chosen by every soul in every dimension. Free will is essential to the bonding and joy of true communion. Consider this.

Because you have free will, you are the one in charge of your own direction and development. You are unique, marvelous, one of a kind. God is not judging you, saying right, wrong, more, less, slow down, or hurry up. These are evaluations you make for yourself. You and your Higher Self interpret your progress.

God wants *every* soul to awaken and to embrace unity with All That Is. Your opportunity to reach this wondrous milestone is not limited to one lifetime. Souls enter and exit planet Earth school at different levels of spiritual development. God is patient, loving, and unceasingly supportive of your ongoing learning and expansion. All life is conscious and will continually evolve. We are divine and our existence is unlimited.

Remember that continually improving your intentional process of living and co-creating with God is more important than any specific goal. Because you are eternal, you will always be in process; you will never reach the end. All learning creates more potential for learning, all love creates more potential for love, and all joy creates further potential for joy. The motives and intentions coming from your heart always affect the reality you experience.

You can focus on keeping your heart open and improving your internal sense of purpose anytime, anywhere. It is not the sooner the better when it comes to your spiritual progress, for there is unlimited time and support available to you. It will happen. However, the sooner you become intentionally active and responsible in your own growth process, the more smoothly and efficiently it can unfold.

Even if your personality has little interest in God or spiritual matters, we can assure you that your Higher Self is very focused in this area. Your Higher Self considers your soul to be a beloved part of your consciousness that has incarnated into the physical world in order to develop and contribute. Along the way you need to heal any insecurities or distorted patterns of behavior that you have developed as a result of experiencing yourself as separate. With God's help, you can heal your emotional wounds and achieve a sense of your individual wholeness. You will then have more to offer in service.

Your Higher Self is dedicated to co-creating your personal contribution to the family of life. At the same time, your individuated soul is continuously seeking reunion with God. These are the reasons you chose to be born. Your Higher Self is constantly providing you with opportunities for healing and accomplishing the spiritual growth you need to reach a higher level of service. Your soul has explored many experiences and points of view, all with the purpose of making a genuine contribution and fully realizing Oneness with all life. Your soul looks forward to living in the profound peace and joy that this realization will bring.

Release any unfavorable judgments about the events and circumstances in your life. Remember that God and a wiser aspect of yourself have allowed these things for your spiritual healing, expansion, and service. Give permission for God and your Higher Self to guide your life without trying to manage everything from the limited perspective of your human personality. Frequently practice opening to your Divine Guidance and honor it with your responsive action.

Accept all beings and all events as they are, even if you wish they were different. When difficulties arise in your life or unfortunate situations in your world come to your attention, begin with prayer. Notice if you are having an emotional reaction. Let go of resistance and be objective rather than judgmental in your observation. The job of your personality is to place attention on your own heart and behavior and to ask God about your best choice concerning what to do next. When you are inspired to seek healing or to work toward change, do your best to let go of the tension that comes from fear or judgment. Put your best effort into what is here right now for you to personally cope with or accomplish. Your next steps will fall into place if you continue to pray and respond to your guidance. Release your concerns into God's care.

Learn to honor yourself and forgive yourself for not seeming perfect. Any sense of unworthiness you may feel comes from self-judgment. There is no need for God to forgive you, because God has never judged you. The real need for forgiveness is from yourself. Acknowledging your mistakes, offering sincere apologies, and making amends may help you reach the peace of self-forgiveness.

Do your best to adopt the viewpoint of your Higher Self. Love yourself, releasing judgment of yourself and others. Trust that each person's challenges and consequences can provide opportunities for developing the strength, compassion, and wholeness needed by that unique individual. No one is a victim. Each individual's sacred experiences eventually will lead to their remembrance of Oneness.

Bless you, beloved friend. We are always nearby. We love you and support you in the free will choices you make. The reality you experience will be the result of your true intentions, as well as your receptivity and responsiveness to God. As you co-create needed changes and healing in your life, your new sense of wholeness and gratitude will lead you to offer yourself to God in service.

> We love you.
> Your Guides and Friends in spirit
> God bless you.

DAY 18

A Loving Heart

Divine Love in your heart helps you stay genuinely present during communication with others. Love listens well, giving full attention in the present moment to the interaction taking place. A loving heart remembers Oneness with the entire family of life and honors the divinity of each individual contributing their perspective.

Love stays open and cares about receiving another person's point of view accurately. Love appreciates that all life is interconnected and does not try to remain separate. A loving heart does not judge or reject. Love accepts all people as they are. Love is respectful, even when there is no agreement.

Love also pays attention when interactions become difficult. Love remains willing to feel honestly what is occurring in any moment, whether it is pleasant or not. A loving heart helps you maintain presence with yourself as well as with others. Love remains available and continues to care. Love remembers personal connections, even after time has passed.

Love does not cling or manipulate. A loving heart feels whole and complete; it then reaches to others for connection and communion. Love recognizes that a variety of moments and experiences are valuable just as they are.

When you are responsive to Divine Love, you honor your own worth as well as the worth of others. Divine Love values your positive motives and growth; it honors your talents, allowing them to expand. God's benevolent Love encourages and supports constructive self-development in all individuals.

A loving heart remains open to learning from a variety of people and events. A loving heart is also receptive to learning from other people's experiences. Episodes in the lives of others do not come to your attention by accident. Furthermore, you will experience more empathy and insight while observing other people if you do not cling to illusions of being different from them or somehow insulated from their circumstances.

Love welcomes what is happening right now, as well as what is possible. Love does not postpone experiencing the fullness, the beauty, or even the pain of any moment. Your willingness to experience *all* feelings is one of the ways you remain present with yourself and with God. When you are feeling stress or emotional pain, a loving heart avoids judgment, distraction, or numbness so that awareness can guide the way to healing. Whispers from

God often come to you through your subtle feelings and intuition. Remaining open to all feelings allows God to guide and work through you in the present moment as your day is actively moving forward.

A loving heart is open and receptive, leading to greater vitality, insight, and responsiveness in personal interactions. Your openness is important for heartfelt connection and intimacy. Receptivity is a strong foundation for your communion with others and with God.

Bless you, dear friend. Those of us in spirit are also learning to maintain loving hearts during every interaction. It is our joy and we hope it will be yours.

Of course, there are times when you need to identify something that is out of order and take appropriate responsible action. Keeping your heart open and free from the constriction of judgment helps you stay receptive to Divine energy and guidance as you respond. This takes practice. We lovingly invite you to try these attitudes of full attention and acceptance in your interactions. Feel the positive results for yourself.

> God supports your practice of staying present and connected.
>
> Your Guides and Friends
>
> Hold love in every moment.

DAY 19

Becoming a Conscious Co-Creator

Divine Love can reach directly into your heart. Love is always near you and available. Deep inside, you are a beautiful being, loving and greatly loved. Your Higher Self hopes for awareness of God's Love to reach every heart. Your soul and your personality can contribute to this widespread fulfillment by learning to co-create with God.

You can become more conscious of Divine Love in your heart and your life when you intentionally attune to your Higher Self. Your sacred Higher Consciousness is already fully aware of God's Love and grand design, but your human personality needs to attune to the higher vibrations of Divine energy and direct knowing. Your receptivity to Divine Guidance will not take your focus away from the realm of physical reality. It will empower you to function more effectively in your world, according to your soul's noble purpose of self-development and contribution.

Consider the spiritual growth that takes place as people go about their business in the physical world. There is a great deal of valuable education and training available on Earth, but the growth we are referring to now is a deeper learning and understanding. Humanity is developing a heartfelt awareness of the Oneness with God that is shared by all life. Many human beings are moving toward willingness to demonstrate profound awareness of Oneness in all their activities.

God expresses through all the magnificent and humble forms of life in Creation; God also *receives* expression through each one. You are not held to an ideal standard of expression. God does not judge you. You are accepted by God and compassionately allowed to be as you are and as you are becoming.

Your Higher Self works to guide you away from illusions of separation and toward personal wholeness and alignment with God. You have been given free will in the hope that you would choose union with God while you are still living in physical reality. Your task is to heal each illusion of helplessness, unworthiness, or separateness *from within that experience.* This challenging journey builds your character and your faith. Your difficulties can provide stimulus to seek God sooner rather than later. Even stress serves you by adding urgency to your efforts to alleviate the suffering of yourself and others.

The illusions encountered in Earth school can be quite convincing. The way to heal any mistaken assumptions you may have is through practicing awareness, honesty, personal responsibility, loving attitudes, and consistent cooperation with God. The qualities you strengthen through your process of self-healing will empower you. You are developing personal mastery.

In order to transcend the illusions that can seem so real, it is necessary to develop your strengths and co-creative approaches to problem solving. These emerging capacities enable you to manifest results in partnership with God. You make your highest contribution to the family of life as you become a conscious co-creator, responsive to divine inspiration. This is the divine design of your soul's journey.

Your individuated soul agreed to incarnate in order to master the fundamentals of co-creating with God. Your deepest desire is to make a new contribution to Creation. As you practice the fundamentals of co-creativity, which are receptivity and responsiveness to God, you are propelled on your spiritual path toward reunion with all life. Rediscovering your Oneness with all will be your own fulfillment as well as God's fulfillment. God loves and appreciates you very much.

Existence in the Light is wonderful beyond what most people now comprehend, but your Higher Self already knows the joy and beauty of living in complete

Love. Your Higher Self tirelessly seeks this peace for your precious soul. Trust your longing to know God, the Source of All That Is. This desire is deep within all of us. Seeking Oneness with the Divine is the most productive function of your soul and your personality. Take the initiative to enrich your personal relationship with God.

You may wonder, "If Oneness is our destiny, why not just wait for it?" or "Why make the effort?" The reason to act now is the need to alleviate suffering. There is a lot of work to be done in order to heal the pain and harshness currently experienced by humanity. There is an urgent necessity in your world for divine alignment and creative solutions. If you are in a body, your soul has chosen to grow and growth cannot be done for you. Strive for personal and planetary peace. It is your deepest need and greatest fulfillment to find your best way to serve.

Progressing intentionally on your path of co-creative contribution can be glorious. There are many miracles and synchronicities to be noticed and enjoyed. Many interactions and revelations are in store for you. There is great potential for the blending of Divine energy with incarnated life that is yet to be experienced in your world. Remember to notice and give thanks for your process of growth and your opportunities to serve. Have loving allowance for yourself and other beings as you continue forward.

Your journey of repeatedly incarnating, healing the

resulting illusions of separateness, and practicing co-creation with God is perfect for your soul's development. This may be difficult for your personality to accept as you struggle with the many challenges of a lifetime. It will make more sense as you give up resistance and focus on solving problems and nurturing harmony. As you practice, you will notice positive results. In turn, positive results help your personality become more trusting and willing. Your devotion to God and willingness to take action will establish a strong foundation.

Life is meant to be a joy and you were meant to participate wholeheartedly. We are happy to join with you if you invite us. Our highest purpose is to radiate and share Divine Love. This is true in every dimension. We will all enjoy fulfillment as the Light of God reaches more hearts.

We love you and our hearts are in tune with your heart. Your growth is our growth, for we are One. Your joy is our joy.

May Heaven and Mother Earth surround you with love, support, and awareness of Divine Oneness during this life and beyond.

> Blessings to you, dear friend,
>
> Your devoted Guides and Friends in spirit
>
> We are part of each other and part of God.

DAY 20

THE GREAT LOVE

The energy of Divine Love is not limited; it can never be used up. Love increases as it is shared. As Love is experienced, by both giving and receiving, it nourishes the growth of more Love.

Jesus, Mohammed, Moses, Krishna, Buddha, and many others came to teach and to share the Love that embraces all beings. God's Great Love includes everyone. Love is with you and within you in every moment.

Welcome the Great Love into your heart and body. Quiet yourself, and then feel the Divine energy surround you, fill you up, and help you feel complete. Notice how Divine Love joins and awakens the love that is already alive within you. Love connects you to all other life, to all of Creation, and to God. It can bring you deep peace. You will feel whole once you realize your divinity and your Oneness with All That Is. This realization is blessed and profoundly joyful. Experiencing the Great Love is God's intention for you. It is your destiny as a soul.

You are constantly nurtured and loved. Your purpose is to seek the Light and to share Divine Love through your personal expression and creativity. The Great Love dwells within all of us. It is magnified when it is cherished and communicated in the unique ways of each spiritual tradition and every form of life.

Our various expressions of Love deepen our connection with Creation. Remember, God expresses Love through you and to you as you experience life. Intentionally support more giving and receiving of spiritual Love. Invite the energy of Divine Love to enhance your every expression of caring, healing, passion, creativity, and service. All your activities can be tremendously enriched as you practice the simple shift of inviting God to blend with you and radiate through you.

We honor you and we are always nearby to add our love to God's blessings. God's guidance and care are yours and ours. We are working to achieve our internal wholeness and unity with all life, just as you are.

We bless you, dear friend. Trust in the wisdom of your heart. Everyone is part of God and connected through God. You are eternal and always loved.

> May peace be with you.
> Your Guides and Friends
> Forever and ever, so it shall be. Amen.

DAY 21

Your Individual Expression

Love touches every life. Love can bring the reality of God into your conscious awareness. God and Divine Love are always present and your creative potential is magnified when you allow them to fill your open heart.

Your spiritual goal is to know God in a personal way and to maintain your own direct divine connection. God wants an invitation to join with you and become a partner in your life. The partnership will be of mutual benefit.

God supports you to be the best you can be, to reach the fullest potential of your magnificent individual expression. God gives and receives Love through you. God does not want to collect your soul as one to be counted. God cherishes your individuality, your kindness, and your beautiful contributions to Creation.

You have an effect on every other being, every atom, and every particle of energy in the vast cosmos. You can be the creator of either a generous or a limited contribution to that great whole. In turn, you receive the expansiveness or contraction of your expression mirrored back to you. You choose your attitudes and responses, and your world reflects the quality of your choices. You are always a creator, never a victim of God or circumstances.

Allow the ever-present Love from God and your loyal Guides to infuse your heart. The gift of totally encompassing Love is available right now. It does not have to be earned; it is your birthright. You are already entitled and deserving of this wondrous Love. Let go of any reluctance to embrace joy and fulfillment now. It will not mean your growth is over, or that there is nothing left to strive for.

All growth, all love, all creativity, and all understandings create further potential for the same. You are eternal and limitless. Like a precious new baby, you are complete as you are, but you are not yet finished. Your possibilities for joyful living, creating, and sharing are unlimited. Your potential for expression is exquisite and infinite.

No one else's essence can take the place of yours. Creation can be compared to a beautiful, intricate woven fabric, with each individual thread important to the texture, color, and design of the cloth. You are wanted and needed, and so are the unique and valuable contributions you will be able to make as you learn to consciously *co-create* them in partnership with God.

Take seriously the importance of your own individual expression and personal responsibility to all life.

We encourage you to request and accept the abundant Love and cooperation of the co-creative community in spirit so close around you. We cherish you and support you in your choices. We want to join with you to enrich our mutual experience and contributions to life.

God blesses us all and rejoices when brotherhood and unity are present in our hearts. We are designed to need and love each other. Our expressions to each other are God sharing with God.

>Bless you,
>
>Your loving Guides and Friends
>
>Our hearts are as one.

DAY 22

KARMA AND CONNECTIONS

God's Love is ready to enter your heart. Your heart is crying out for Love to come in. So why is opening yourself to receive Divine Love sometimes difficult? You may need to first believe that you deserve to be loved. Know that God has limitless Love and acceptance for every being in Creation, including you.

God's Love is always around you, hoping to be allowed in, no matter what you have or have not done. Love is available for you, regardless of any mistakes or unfortunate decisions you may have made using your free will. God does not punish or condemn. However, God does allow you to experience consequences and karma to support your learning and authentic growth. At the same time, God holds deep compassion for anyone who is suffering. We are all God's children.

You are not a victim of any unhealed condition within yourself. You are not a victim of any person, event, or circumstance. Furthermore, from the highest spiritual perspective, no one else is a victim of you. Whatever occurs in physical reality has been chosen or consented to by the Higher Self of each individual involved, according to the sacred purpose of their soul. This seems difficult to believe considering some of the harsh conditions and events on planet Earth, but be assured that this is true.

Your goal as an evolving soul is to realize your Oneness with all life and to achieve true spiritual union with God. It may take a variety of experiences to dissolve all your judgmental feelings of separateness from other individuals and their difficulties. It may not be easy to eliminate your notions of invulnerability to the wounds and disadvantages that others experience, but it is very important. Genuine compassion leads to an open heart, which is essential for the elevation of your consciousness.

Sometimes the only way to heal an illusion that you are immune or separate from someone else's experience is to have a similar experience yourself. The experience could occur in this life or in another incarnation. You are eternal, so time and even death are not obstacles to accomplishing your learning. You have time for every situation your soul needs to experience. You create every encounter you need in order to confirm for yourself that God is always with you and within you.

Karma is whatever experience you need for your spiritual progress. Karma may involve experiences that seem to your personality to be fortunate, synchronistic, or healing, as well as those that seem painful or challenging. You have drawn both types of experience to yourself as opportunities for new insight and forward movement. Karma is not reward or punishment. There is no judgment involved in karma.

Karma is simply a reflection, a situation that can be supportive of your insight and next steps. It is helpful if you can stay alert to recognize this principle when something either positive or problematic occurs. You know what to do; proceed with your prayers, receptivity, and action. Ask for Divine Guidance and Right Order as you continue. You are always loved and your journey through your incarnations is always supported.

Love yourself along the way. Respect your soul for your willingness to attempt growth in every lifetime, whether or not it seems enjoyable. Know that the plan for your incarnation and the further expansion of your soul is unfolding continuously and purposefully. It cannot be otherwise.

Consider the entire journey of your soul. You will have many opportunities in a variety of realities to accomplish your desired spiritual progress. Have faith in God and in the brilliance of God's plan. The Divine Plan is so remarkable that it deserves celebration. Celebrate the approaching end of guilt, regret, and blame. Celebrate the promise of inner peace and rejoicing.

Look forward to the future with anticipation of contribution, fulfillment, and loving communion. These are the aspirations of your soul and your soul will attain them. As a human being, you influence the timing and circumstances of your growth and accomplishments by your personal attitudes and free will choices. You have the right and the need to make your own choices and then to experience the results of those choices. This leads to your authentic learning.

It is Divine Law that the free will of every being is to be respected, without interference. Autonomy is important for each individual's spiritual progress to be genuine. Claim your personal sovereignty. You can request God's protection from any outside interference with you.

When you open your heart to allow more love and connection, this may include opening to the love and connection available from beyond your physical reality. If you seek contact with other dimensions, you have the right and the responsibility to set specific boundaries regarding what type of contacts you are willing to accept. If you *always* make your spiritual connections *through God*, you can be safe opening to contact beyond the physical realm. The Guides and Friends who are in active co-creation with God are not offended if you care for yourself with prayers for protection and discernment. Be consistent with this responsibility.

You can also pray for the upliftment and healing of any malevolence or interference affecting you.

If you wish for the love and blessings available from God, the angelic realms, and other dimensions to assist you as you face your challenges, then simply ask. Let your free will be known through prayer. Just soften your heart and ask to receive only Divine Guidance and connections *approved by God for this moment in time.* This is blessed. You are welcome to everything that those of us who serve as Spirit Guides offer to share, for it is our purpose and pleasure to relay Divine energy to you. We also strive for full remembrance of Oneness.

Bless you, dear friend. We love you constantly. Our wish is for you to receive Love from us and from within yourself as well, for God dwells within every one of us.

> All is perfect.
>
> Your Guides and Friends in spirit
>
> You are respected and treasured.

DAY 23

Feelings and Personal Responsibility

Love sees into your heart. God knows the pain, the sorrow, and the insecurity that sometimes dwell there, even when you attempt to conceal these feelings from yourself and others. Divine Love understands and allows your feelings to be present without judgment and without demanding change.

Take time to experience your feelings honestly, whatever they may be. Feelings, which are neither right nor wrong, are an important element of your humanity. Your emotional reactions can provide clues about what is really going on deep inside you. There is no need to suppress or numb uncomfortable feelings such as embarrassment, depression, jealousy, fear, or anger, but it is very important to behave responsibly. Any attempt to ignore feelings comes from denial or self-criticism, attitudes that are counterproductive to the active process of healing into personal wholeness.

When facing your difficult feelings, you have the choice of whether to indulge in an emotional reaction or to reconnect with God and respond more constructively. All your feelings can ultimately lead you to joy and fulfillment, but you need to honestly identify them and seek healing when you need it. Genuine healing cannot occur when some feelings, which may be painful, unpleasant, or socially unacceptable, are denied or disguised.

Acknowledgment of your feelings combined with personal responsibility contributes to healing. Taking responsibility for yourself involves asking God for help. You may also need help from a therapist or another qualified person whom you trust. Doing the work of self-healing could be an important part of your purpose in this lifetime.

If you have been actively working on healing uncomfortable feelings, you will realize you are succeeding in resolving an issue when it does not trigger the same intensity of distress. You will no longer need to use effort and willpower to control those reactions. You will notice that an internal shift has taken place; the unhealed energy you carried has been uplifted by Divine Grace in response to your awareness and integrity.

Remember, it is not the sooner the better when it comes to your spiritual progress, just the sooner the easier. If your personality chooses to avoid or refuse opportunities to use your feelings as a guide to truth, that choice remains the right of your free will. Nevertheless, your Higher Self is directly in touch with the areas of growth that your soul has scheduled for this incarnation. Your Higher Self will work to lovingly and repeatedly offer your personality new opportunities to accomplish the self-awareness and course corrections your soul is seeking.

If you continue to postpone your opportunities to explore feelings and heal your wounds, misunderstandings, or counterproductive behaviors, you may feel stuck or blocked in some area of your life. In that case, your Higher Self, with infinite and tender love for your soul and your personality, will continue to design situations that could motivate you to take action toward the change you need. Your ego may find it increasingly difficult to avoid the opportunities you will have in the future to accept personal responsibility.

If this still does not work, your Higher Self can collaborate with your physical body to call you home to the embrace of God. During the interval between lifetimes, you can recover and make new plans for your next attempt to accomplish the growth your soul is seeking. You will have spiritual advisors to help you plan conditions and companions for your next incarnation in the hope that they might be more effective at facilitating the willingness and healing you need.

This is not to say that everyone entering the transition you call death has unfinished business regarding their purpose for that lifetime. Most people who enter the transition back to spirit have accomplished their goals for that incarnation, even if they are very young. Some people have a shorter agenda for learning or contributing within the circumstances of a specific family, culture, gender, or period in history that they have chosen for that lifetime. A life plan is for an individual's Higher Self and soul to determine and evaluate together.

If you feel certain that you already know all your answers or you have grown all you are willing to, then you should put your earthly affairs in order. If your soul had learned everything you wanted to learn, you would have no further need to remain in your physical body. If you are still alive on Earth, there is positive potential for your remaining time.

Respect and love yourself for your willingness to incarnate and work on the personal growth and inner healing that you need. Your soul is striving to develop the qualities and practices of an effective co-creator with God. Have loving allowance for your stumbles and periods of difficulty. Everything contributes to your spiritual learning.

Always remember that you are never alone. You can call on God and the gentle spiritual beings around you to support you in all your experiences. They have endless patience and compassion for you as you explore your human feelings. They have heartfelt love for you. The support is yours. Believe this and open to it gladly.

You are *eternal* and limitless. You are not going to run out of time to reach the goal of your soul, which is to complete a loving, productive, and fulfilling Journey of Return to God and Oneness. Even after coming into full awareness of Oneness, you will never reach the end of your immortal existence. All your love, generate more potential within you for your ongoing contributions.

> God bless you and keep you.
> Your Guides and Friends in spirit
> You are always deeply loved.

DAY 24

Your Personal Sovereignty

Love and truth are both qualities of God. God encourages you to be in touch with the Divine Love and truth within yourself, for these are qualities of your own divinity.

God dwells within you and speaks to you through your awareness of the Love and truth you sense within your heart. Learn to trust this sacred communication and respond to it without hesitation.

You are designed to receive your best guidance from within. You can also gain considerable spiritual insight from situations and human interactions in your life. These are best understood after checking with your own deep feelings and with your personal values of Love and truth. You are sovereign. Becoming the authority for yourself regarding your life choices is both your right and your personal responsibility.

Do not expect any single person or doctrine to provide all the answers about what is appropriate or inappropriate for you. Seek wisdom, teachers, and practices that can help you discover your own answers.

Appreciate that you are a unique and independent being who has free will and a spark of divinity within you. Purify your intention to align your personal will with the Will of God. Frequently opening to Divine Guidance and willingly responding brings you into personal partnership with God. This direct divine alignment enables you to successfully co-create with God, finding your personal fulfillment in service to the Divine Plan.

Your Higher Self is intimately familiar with the goals your soul has planned, hoped for, and worked toward in this lifetime. On the other hand, your conscious mind might be less in touch with your divine purpose. Your personality may even think you have other priorities until you feel a stirring within yourself that suggests your life could be working better or that there is something more you want to seek.

Discovering who you are as a soul requires openness and focused intention. You can bring your inner knowledge about your life purpose and best direction into conscious awareness if you take time to attune and pray for help. Abundant support is available from God, your Higher Self, and the Master Teachers and Servers of the Light that your heart resonates with at this time.

As you call on these sacred sources of support and guidance, continue to go within your own heart to verify for yourself the validity of each insight and inspiration. Do not feel you must accept every teaching from any source, no matter how close to you they are or how widely known and revered. With prayerful consideration, determine if a specific teaching or intuitive impression resonates with the sense of Love and truth deep within you.

As you tune in to the deeper feelings and responses within your heart, you will expand your ability to discern what is appropriate for you. Learn to notice these insistent or subtle inner responses and to trust them as direct communication with your Higher Consciousness.

You are a child of God, capable of attunement to Divine Guidance, which is available through stillness, prayer, and receptivity. We hope you will be receptive to other people, too. The physical companions on your spiritual journey may also serve as your guides and teachers as you experience life together.

God bless you and keep you. You are never alone because you always have help and guidance available. Trust yourself in your search for truth. You are divine, and God dwells within you. You are sovereign and complete as you are, but not yet finished.

> We bless your continued progress.
> Your Guides and Friends in spirit
> We applaud you.

DAY 25

Individuation and Return

God's Love, the Great Love, is the Source of the energy present in all Creation. Love is essential to understanding the organization and dynamics of the universe. Love is the connection. Love is the motivation for Creation and more Love will be the outcome.

Your soul has chosen your lifetimes as you would choose classes. Each physical incarnation provides an environment that is particularly well suited for learning what you need at a specific stage in your soul's development.

Your Higher Self exists in the reality of Oneness with God and all life. You are connected with All That Is. A portion of your Higher Consciousness individuated and your soul was born, becoming a unique and precious *individual* consciousness. Your goal was to experience and develop a distinct perspective as an individual in order to make your personal valuable contribution to Creation. It is important for you to recognize and appreciate your intended purpose.

As the way to develop full awareness of your power, responsibility, and importance as an individual, you have accepted some temporary illusions of separation from the rest of Creation. You have entered your experience of individuality with the sacred intention of becoming the best that you can be and sharing the most that you can share. As a soul, you are seeking to co-create your contribution to the family of life in partnership with God.

While you are living physically on Earth, you are in the process of learning to value and nurture the marvelous being that you are. You are learning to develop integrity with your Higher Self and to appreciate your human self. This becomes an opportunity for appreciating others and their challenges and contributions. It leads to your awareness of our mutual divinity and to opening your heart to unity among the family of life.

We offer you this foundational understanding: Creation expands and evolves as we develop ourselves and then give something back to the whole. Our spiritual evolution progresses from existence in a blissful state of Oneness to individuation as souls, development of our unique contributions, and achievement of our commitment to the highest good for all life. Then we are ready to rejoin and enhance Oneness. This is the Journey of Return that engages each one of us.

Oneness, which is our collective consciousness, is enhanced as it absorbs the awareness and gifts added by each individual. Our contributions add to the expansion and refinement of Oneness; every enrichment is the result of a soul's co-creative cooperation with God.

You are learning to respect and validate yourself, to discover and develop what is uniquely yours. This step cannot be skipped in your quest for union with God. When you fully value yourself, realizing that you are part of God and all Creation, you become ready to genuinely love others. You realize that they are also part of you and part of God. You naturally want to co-create in partnership with God and share in service to life around you. This is how you can participate in the Divine Plan.

As you learn to honor yourself, it feels safer and more fulfilling to open your heart to others. When you feel more complete, you are able to reach out to others with greater compassion and generosity. When you understand your own worthiness and permanent place of belonging in the family of life, a deep peace settles into your heart.

As you become secure in your self-love, you become willing to let go of judgment and any need to feel insulated from difficulties and differences around you. Your appreciation of your personal divinity and Oneness with everything is deepened as you develop and share your creative contributions.

We support you in your quest to embody unconditional love and to choose unity with all life. We are on the same rewarding journey ourselves and we will all succeed. It is destined.

Bless you, dear one. Love is yours for the asking. Soften your heart and open yourself to receive Divine Love.

> God is always with you.
>
> Your Guides and Friends in other dimensions
>
> Everything is alive. Everything is Divine, and all is One.

DAY 26

THE TAPESTRY OF CREATION

Love embraces you. Just as your physical body is surrounded by the air you breathe, your soul is surrounded by God's Love and support. Just as you allow air into your lungs, let Divine Love come into your heart to nourish and sustain you.

Divine Love gives rise to Creation. Fascinating patterns of events and interactions are endlessly created within the fabric of Creation by many beings. Divine energies influence the direction of Creation's evolvement according to God's plan. Even if your personality does not find all the patterns pleasing, realize that they are all woven with a purpose from strands of Love. Every detail has an important place in the intricate design, which is magnificent and holy.

The fabric of Creation is divinely conceived and coordinated in its unfoldment. Evidence of God's continuous orchestration of Creation's evolvement is becoming increasingly apparent in your reality. The living tapestry of Love is breathtaking in its structure, power, and complexity.

The tapestry symbolizes the grand design and potential of God's intention for Creation. Every color in the spectrum is woven into this cloth. Each shade, line, and curve, as well as every flaw and texture, is valuable for the contribution it makes to the entire design. Every event and experience augments Creation. All the free will choices and actions by individuals have effects that are integrated into the evolving design.

God continually updates the Divine Plan in response to the current intentions, actions, and needs of individuals. God's design accommodates the factor of our free will, which is essential for our spiritual progress to be authentic. The alignment and interaction of our personal will with the Will of God determines how both free will and fate play a part in our soul's journey. Even though our destiny of reunion with God remains constant, we have a substantial influence on our steps to get there. With infinite wisdom and Love, God is adjusting the Divine Plan for our benefit even in this present moment.

Remember that your place in the grand design is significant. You would not be here in a physical body right now if it were not important. Pay attention to your relationships, your spiritual practice, and your service. Appreciate the emphasis and subtlety that the threads of your life add to this wondrous tapestry of Creation as they interweave with the threads of others.

Does one thread obscure another in a woven fabric? No, each one is meant to go over, under, around, and between the others. No strand is covered by another for more than a moment in this constantly fluid dance of interaction. Each thread is meant to be whole and strong. Each one has a part to play, a sacred contribution to make.

Every color is a precious gift. Purple can provide richness and depth; yellow can bloom in golden glory. Red can burst forth as accent and stimulus. Green contributes contrast and connection. Blue may add serenity and radiance. All the colors are important to the composition.

It would not make sense for any color to dim its own brilliance, hesitant to overwhelm the others. It would be counterproductive for yellow to change its appearance to become reddish because of its admiration for red. That would leave the tapestry with an overabundance of orange, and without the sweet light shade of yellow where it is needed.

Trust in the Divine Plan for your life. Trust the potential of the gifts and the challenges that you are blessed with in this incarnation. Accept your unique traits. Develop your relationships and talents; each one has a purpose in your life. Remember that you are always loved and honored by God, and it is important for you to appreciate and care for the special person that you are.

You are in the process of discovering which precious colors and textures you are contributing to the expanding tapestry of Creation. You are learning to value your personal qualities, allowing the expression of their originality and authenticity. Dare to be as intense and vivid as neon! Be willing to be as delicate and subtle as a soft pastel. You are beautiful and needed as you are now and as you will become.

> Bless you. You are so dearly loved and treasured.
>
> Your Guides and Friends in spirit
>
> We are with you this very minute.

DAY 27

INDIVIDUAL RIGHTS AND RESPONSIBILITIES

Love is reaching out to you as you are reaching out for Love. Divine Love is here for you. Open your heart to gratefully receive it. Allow the exquisite loving vibrations surrounding you to saturate and nourish you.

There is no need to feel separate from others or from Love. Your feelings of separateness can be healed. We are all One. We are simply individual expressions of the same magnificent Divine Love and creative power.

You give as you radiate Love and you can receive the emanation of Love as well. You draw God's supportive Love to yourself, and you also receive it through the expression of others. Throughout your evolution as a soul, you attract whatever energies and encounters are timely for you to experience.

Others involved in your interactions are also experiencing what is appropriate and necessary for their growth. These encounters are what you might call "matches made in Heaven." The soul of each individual involved has agreed to enter into your mutual experiences and explorations. The agreements and the first linkages with each other are made by your Higher Selves.

You are often unaware of continually being the creator of your own reality. This misperception is the reason you might sometimes feel resistance, upset, or discouragement regarding the experiences you face. Sometimes you may feel compelled from within yourself to seek various experiences or to explore certain interactions without your rational mind understanding a reason. This is your spiritual creativity at work. Your Higher Self, not your personality, is leading the way. Your human self can then choose your attitude and response to the situation. This is your right of free will.

All souls have a need to explore the experiences and interactions most appropriate for their growth at any specific time. These happenings may be interpreted as positive or negative by the individual involved, according to their personal perceptions and emotional reactions.

Your Higher Self sees all experiences as positive because of what they can teach you. Your life experiences are designed to eventually lead to personal healing and unconditional love for yourself and others. You attract specific circumstances, events, and encounters according to your current needs as a soul and personality. Your external reality provides reflections to you, clues about the state of your internal self and what you need to do. Your experiences and deep feelings are meant to lead you to greater awareness of your Oneness with others and all life. Life can be full of joy and productivity when you flow with the ever-present divine energies, allowing synchronicities to gently sweep you along.

You have built-in guidance constantly available from within yourself. Open to your Divine Guidance through sincere practices of prayer and humble receptivity. Initiating communion with Divine Wisdom is your responsibility as an aspiring co-creator with God. Learn to trust your internal guidance; respond to it without hesitation. Your best guidance comes from God through your Higher Consciousness, not from your personality or an outside authority. You always have free will and the right to make your own choices. It is time to claim personal sovereignty and responsibility for yourself and to consistently allow the same for others.

Each person's Higher Self knows exactly what to do and why. However, it is necessary for a human personality to willingly attune to their spiritual purpose, discovering it through stillness and prayer. A soul is still learning and healing karma; there may be emotional pain or misunderstandings that need to be resolved at the personality level. But each soul has noble intentions of learning to co-create with God or the incarnation would not have occurred.

As a soul, you have agreed to come into a physical body to pursue the spiritual growth and contribution that you hope to accomplish. Living in a physical body, feeling the necessity for food, shelter, and safety requires the development of self-responsibility in order to survive. The particular circumstances and experiences of your lifetime can focus your attention on the specific learning that is the immediate priority of your soul.

As your personality aligns with your soul's mission, you will develop a grateful willingness to respond to your intuition. You will know that your life is on track and that you are moving in your best direction. As you experience your sense of purpose and the peace of your inner knowing, it is important to allow other people to enjoy a similar freedom.

Resisting the divine flow of occurrences in your life or refusing responsibility may lead to struggle or emotional pain. God and your Higher Self have great wisdom and perspective in these areas. Consider consistently cooperating with them to see an improvement in how you feel.

The way of attunement is not meant to be difficult, but it does take practice for most people. There is clarity and abundant loving help available if you are willing to ask for it.

If your personality uses free will to decline your most beneficial lessons, those decisions will be respected and supported by God and the loving beings around you. With great wisdom, patience, and Love, your Higher Self will continue to provide new opportunities for healing and understanding. There will be more chances for your personality to engage in the experiences and interactions that you need in your pursuit of harmony with all Creation.

Your soul's level of evolvement determines which lessons are necessary. Your personality's choices of attitudes and actions affect the timing and the form of each lesson. If you delay, the circumstances and cast of characters involved in your lesson may change, but your soul's need for a certain understanding or healing remains a priority until it is accomplished. If you continue to refuse opportunities that are needed by your soul, you will probably find that later opportunities to practice and grow are more intense and more difficult to avoid.

This is true even if you carry the need for specific lessons beyond one incarnation and into another lifetime. You can be sure that your Higher Self offers great wisdom and constant support as you pursue remembrance of Oneness. Your Higher Consciousness continually designs your opportunities for personal mastery and for healing any remaining illusions of separateness until you are successful. And you will succeed. It is blessed and guaranteed by God, but the ease and timing are greatly influenced by your willingness.

We offer you love and support in your quest. You only need to call on us. We seek our connection with God, our wholeness, and union with all life, just as you do. Let us seek and serve together.

>   Bless you, dear heart. We love you and are always near.
>
>   Your Guides and Friends on the spirit side
>
>   We pray to God, too.

DAY 28

Mastery of Sacred Creativity

Do not hesitate to embrace Divine Love. Love is already embracing you. Your willing immersion in the energy of Love accelerates your advancement to the profound peace of recognizing your deep connection with all life.

The energy of Divine Love attracts and reassures you. It supports and guides you as you make progress toward your remembrance of Oneness with all life. The flow of sacred Love can fill your being, empowering, healing, and transforming you. The effect of Divine Love becomes even more powerful when you give God your permission to be an active influence in your life. This process is blessed.

Your Higher Self is the spark of God that already dwells within you. You do not need to search outside yourself to find it. Your body is one of many physical forms that contain the essence of God. You are holy; appreciate and honor the divine quality within yourself.

Allow your natural divinity to shine through your open heart.

As you realize that God is part of you, remember that you are also part of God. This fact is the basis of the reality of Oneness. We are inseparable, already One. We are simply individual expressions or facets of a glorious collective that includes all life.

Your Higher Consciousness, in collaboration with God, chose to extend part of your essence into the illusion of separation from the completeness and security of existing in Oneness. You were willing to enter the challenging experience of becoming an individuated soul because of your deep desire to share your Love with the totality of Creation. In order to create your personal contribution to Oneness, you had to temporarily accept the illusion of separateness and experience yourself as an individual.

Experiencing yourself as a separate being can sometimes feel painful, lonely, or insecure. At other times it feels exciting, creative, and empowering. In any case, individuation is the important beginning step in your soul's evolvement. Living as an individual assists you in developing self-responsibility as nothing else could. Individuality creates the need to repeatedly initiate your personal connection with God.

Self-responsibility and steady alignment with God are the essentials for working your way out of the illusions of separateness. Both are necessary for acknowledging and healing every judged or disowned part of your consciousness. Healing the aspects of yourself that are in a condition of distress or dysfunction is needed for coming into *wholeness* as an individual. You will then be able to offer your healthy confident wholeness back to God as you lovingly share yourself in service.

Your difficult and convincing illusions of your separateness have a very important spiritual purpose and are actually serving you. To meet the challenges they present, you need to develop personal responsibility, purity of intention, and willingness to be in consistent partnership with God. *These are the very same qualities both your soul and your personality need to maintain for you to become a trustworthy co-creator.*

Your actions of service in response to Divine Guidance are the foundation for the flowering of your natural spiritual abilities. These exceptional capacities can include intuition, healing ability, extraordinary perception, creative talents, and manifestation. The more you serve, the more capabilities you are granted to enhance and support your service. This spiritual expansion beyond the limits of your five physical senses becomes more possible and appropriate as you demonstrate unwavering commitment to God and willingness to follow God's guidance with action. A co-creator aligns their personal will with the Will of God in order to create in harmony with the Divine Plan. This alignment facilitates the original goal of your Higher Self, which is the development of your sacred creativity in service to the elevation of consciousness.

It is important to appreciate your uniqueness as you become a constructive co-creator. The goal of your incarnation is to consciously practice your co-creativity in partnership with God. To completely develop the innovative contributions you are capable of making, you will need to honor and respond to your most altruistic motives.

Your soul has spent eons studying how you are the creator of your reality and how the current state of your inner consciousness is reflected to you from your surroundings. As you notice causes and effects in your life and become willing to heal your personal issues, you are seeking to dissolve your illusion of being separate. Living as an individual has helped you understand how you are creating and what you hope to heal.

People differ widely in their comprehension of the dynamics of internal cause and outward result, but this awareness is fundamental to mastery of sacred creativity. Results in your life experience are generated not only by your attitudes and behavior, but also by your intentions and integrity.

In spirit, the effects of your attitudes, beliefs, and intentions are instantaneous. However, when you incarnate into your dimension of physical space and time, things seem to be slowed down. You perceive the consequences of your attitudes and actions as sequential. Whether the effects are noticed immediately or sometime in the future, the cause is followed by the result.

The interval of time in your dimension between a cause and its result is a great help in your learning process. However, there have been some dire developments in Earth experience due to the intense but necessary illusions of separateness that exist in physical reality. Some unfortunate choices have been made by people who felt insecure, defensive, angry, selfish, or unconcerned about the profound impact their intentions and actions could have. We do not need to list the painful examples that exist in your world.

Realize that it is now time for Divine energy and awareness of Oneness to become more influential in your reality. As you develop inner wholeness through spiritual integrity and deep personal healing, the Love in your heart will prevail. Your blossoming wholeness will lead to greater accomplishment and heartfelt brotherhood.

The coming decades will find people working cooperatively to make a contribution while healing their illusions of separateness at the same time. The qualities of devotion to God, solidarity with others, and inspired creativity, existing all together, will establish and nourish many positive projects and environments. These developments will foster innovation, noble expression, and gratitude within individuals as never before.

You have entered a new millennium, one with the exciting potential for widespread personal responsibility and Divine Right Order to manifest in your reality. Those of us in spirit rejoice with you. We join with you in loving communion and in service to the unfolding of these long-awaited developments. We offer help in your process of personal healing as well as support for your planetary transformation.

We bless you and love you dearly. Our aspiration is to serve God and embrace unity. We love God and ourselves, and we wish the same fulfillment for you.

> In Oneness,
>
> Your Guides and Friends in spirit
> We wish you the joy and peace of
> remembering who you really are.

DAY 29

EMBODIMENT AND TRANSMISSION OF DIVINE ENERGY

Limitless Love can be yours. Divine Love surrounds you at every moment and hopes for you to invite it into your heart. Love wants to combine with you. It is ready to infuse your being, to blend with your physical body and become one with you.

Every cell of your body longs to be in the presence of Love, receiving Love and expressing Love. God hopes that you will feel so loved and so loving that your life will be fulfilled and generous.

As you open your receptivity and incorporate more Divine energy into your physical body, you will notice that this process has a healing and uplifting effect on you. It raises your vibration. As you practice, you will become increasingly aware of your own spiritual abilities and your personal capacity to share the energy of God's Love. You will sense your life purpose and become interested in who you are as a soul. With dedication and joy, you will discover and develop your strengths and make your special contribution to your world. You are a gift.

Recognizing and developing yourself can be like composing and singing a song of praise to Heaven. Allowing Divine Love to flow through you and sharing yourself with an open heart is offering the most precious gift you can give. Everyone will be fortunate to receive the benefit of your loving contribution.

The Light of God is everywhere, available for every person to absorb and embody. Physically receive the energy emanating from God. Willingly take it in, for it is as vital to you as the air you breathe. Divine Love purifies as it nourishes and sustains you. It refines the sensitivities and abilities of your humanity. The Light expands as the flow of energy is received and shared. Channeling the stream of Divine energy is a blessing and an act of service; be grateful to participate.

Embrace your process of recognizing and honoring the beautiful being that you are and you will make great progress in your earnest quest to know God. God is within you and within all others. When the deep realization of this reaches your heart, it will seem to be obvious and a revelation at the same time.

When you truly value the divinity in yourself and others, it becomes easy to feel profound wonder, reverence, and connection with all of Creation. If you want to share Divine energy with life around you, repeatedly establish your intentional *divine alignment*. Open your heart and make a personal direct connection with God. Remember to ground, purposely connecting your energy with planet Earth, for Earth is where you have chosen to live and serve at this time. Allow the fullness of Light to blend with you, to expand and pour through you. Become a conduit.

You can broadcast Light, the presence and benevolence of God. Because you are in service, the Earth happily supports you in this sharing. *Embody* Divine Light, invite it to enrich your personal energy and inspire your creative expression. Allow Light to flow through you, to radiate outward, and to penetrate into the Earth and planetary situations as a contribution to your physical dimension.

Purifying your own energy field through processes of personal healing enhances your ability to transmit Divine energy. Every time you bring healing to an aspect of wounding or distortion within yourself, you are building your own capacity to physically relay the sacred energy and its benefits to life around you. Your heart can become an open door, allowing more Divine Love and healing to enter your physical dimension. By bringing in Divine energy, you can elevate the vibrational matrix for everyone. Thank God for the blessing of this holy radiance.

Sometimes you may pray for healing and then experience a download of sacred energy in response.

At other times Light may stream through your body unexpectedly. When this merging occurs, renew your divine alignment, ground yourself, then relax and allow the current of energy to flow into your dimension as the Will of God directs it.

The transmission of healing energy from God may follow the trajectory of your compassion, addressing what you are concerned about, but it is not the job of your personal will to determine what result is needed. Attempting to control the dynamic or feeling overly responsible for the outcome can create internal tension, constricting the free flow of Divine energy through you. Open your heart in gratitude, relax your body, and just allow the blending. Channeling Light is a beautiful activity of co-creation with God and a profound service to life around you. Surrender the management and results of the healing into God's care.

Love to you, dear friend. You are blessed and loved by God and a multitude of benevolent beings. Remember that your own essence is Love. We cherish our contact with you, and we grow as you grow. We all create greater potential in this process.

> Go your way in joy and harmony. Bless you.
> Your many Guides and Friends in spirit
> We love you.

DAY 30

Your Personal Journey

Genuine love can guide you. Notice the feelings of sincere love and willingness to serve that you find within your heart. You do not need to understand everything. It is more important to allow love for yourself and for any facet of God's Creation to thrive with pure intent and nurturing care.

Divine energies can draw you into a beautiful loving vibration if you are relaxed and open. Take responsibility for your divine alignment. Devote time to your spiritual practice of stillness and receptivity. Intentionally connect with God and the Earth at the same time to support your discernment and sense of safety. Then, if it feels right to you, stay open to experiences that may be unfamiliar. Trust in the wisdom of God and your Higher Self to lead you on the pathway toward your greatest growth and fulfillment.

You planned the direction of your incarnation before you were born. Your soul received guidance from your Higher Self and God in planning your priorities for this lifetime. Your Higher Self holds the compass and is able to see farther ahead than your personality can see. Therefore, trust your Higher Consciousness and God to guide you. The route has been carefully and lovingly designed to lead you through the experiences that best support your spiritual progress.

However, there are many forks in the road, and your personality is in the position to decide which way to proceed. This is your free will in action. You will be allowed to make these choices even if they lead to danger, detours, or dead ends. The practice of going into your heart to seek Divine Guidance at every significant decision point is very important. This will enable you to choose the most productive and enriching directions for your soul's purpose.

You have a best path designed to support your personal growth and contribution. Resistance or refusal on your path can lead to emotional discomfort, confusion, and loss of momentum. You may feel a sense of struggle or lack of purpose. If this occurs, your Higher Self will be busy trying to get your attention to encourage you to self-correct.

Your Higher Self will be drawing experiences into your life designed to foster your willingness to choose again, to make a better decision for yourself regarding the next steps that are most appropriate for you. Your own best path may appear rocky and challenging, while many people you know seem to be strolling along smooth highways. However, this may only be your personality's perception. Remember, your personality is not the part of you with the compass and the long-distance vision.

Resistance to your circumstances or your calling often intensifies any difficulty. If you are on your most appropriate path, you will have a sense of positive direction, even if there are challenges to overcome. If you are taking time to attune to your inner guidance when making a choice, you will feel the validity of your decisions. Your best path will ultimately lead you to more growth and fulfillment.

Surrendering to your Divine Guidance is not the same as becoming passive. Sometimes it means accepting responsibility to extend help or friendship, to seek healing, or to speak your truth. Your Divine Guidance may also inspire you to create something original or to work toward important changes in your life or your world.

Your journey may take you steeply uphill at times, but the environment and encounters could be especially interesting to you. Your path may present obstacles, but you will find that every barrier can be overcome if you ask for the help you need. The process of moving through specific difficulties will help you build important strengths and skills that are essential for developing your contributions. You will learn to appreciate your individuality and to accept the challenge and responsibility of this guided way of learning.

Do not compare your path to the paths of others. Be assured that your soul's journey will eventually lead you to awareness of our Oneness within the embrace of God, no matter how many detours you may choose. Love your companions and help each other when your paths cross or run parallel for a time. Join hands in respect, intimacy, and friendship; savor the loving, creative, and thrilling moments. Cherish the many friends you meet and be willing to release their hands when your paths diverge, knowing that different experiences and new companions await each of you. Remember that physical presence is not necessary for the love between you to remain.

We are all One. Each of us will find our own way of reaching our realization of sacred Oneness with God and all life. We will support each other and learn together in the process.

We bless you, dear friend, and we respect your sovereign choices. We are steadfast in our support for you. We invite you to call on us and *always on God* for needed strength and guidance. Our journeys are blessed and divinely guided.

In brotherhood and solidarity,

Your Guides and Friends in spirit

We wish you enthusiasm and contentment at the same time.

And always Love.

DAY 31

Your Perfectly Designed Life

Love is involved in an outreach to all humanity. The energy of Divine Love surrounding you and your planet is expanding every day. It will lead to your deepest peace and fulfillment if you allow this sacred Love to dwell in your heart. Receive the Love God has for you, then be willing to intentionally share it through your personal expression.

You have chosen to be who you are in this lifetime. Your soul has excellent reasons for choosing your gender, your family, the cultures and religions you have been exposed to, and the people you have encountered. With guidance from your Higher Self and your Spirit Guides, you as a soul chose which of your talents and areas of needed healing to focus on in this incarnation.

You may notice upsets and disadvantages in the circumstances of your life. You may even hold resentment or hurt feelings about the challenges you have faced.

However, your Higher Self considers these influences to be providing helpful opportunities for developing compassion, resourcefulness, and acceptance of yourself and others. The events in your life provide repeated opportunities to accept responsibility, to build relationships, and to pursue personal healing. Your life experiences are opportunities carefully designed especially for you. They are stepping-stones toward your joyful realization of Oneness with all life.

Take an objective look at your current situation and relationships with these things in mind. What have your particular circumstances in planet Earth school contributed to your spiritual development and to your desire to be of service? What is the greatest potential a soul could attain by living your life? What growth and contributions are possible if you choose to listen and respond to God each day?

Become aware of the lessons you are working on as well as your areas of potential. What do you hope to improve in yourself or in this world before you return to your natural and familiar nonphysical state as spirit? What would you like to have accomplished when the time comes to graduate from your current class in Earth school?

God and your Higher Self are absolutely brilliant to have created you just as you are and to be drawing to you the specific people, crises, and opportunities that appear in your life. Notice the wisdom at work in the planning of your incarnation. If you would like additional insight about the purpose and progress of your life, we encourage you to pray and meditate. Ask God for clarification. The request for clarity is beneficial because it will help you choose your responses to your experiences. Your personal choices and responses affect the intensity and timing of your spiritual development.

If you want to understand more about yourself and your possibilities, pay attention to the clues that appear around you. These insights may come to you through communications, observations, events, or people who touch your life. You may be presented with new opportunities for practicing your skills or exploring new directions. The awareness you seek may come to you as intuition, imagination, or even as a random thought that at first seems to be insignificant. Notice and consider these signs.

Recognize the possible significance of these clues and bits of guidance. Pray for God to help you discern what is valuable. Your willing service to the Divine Plan involves learning to notice the support coming to you as whispers of Divine Guidance. Give yourself permission to act on your intuition. Nothing that happens is accidental. Fortunate coincidences are actually synchronicities, gifts from God that provide encouragement or open the way for you. Synchronicities, intuition, and your heartfelt dedication to your personal direction can confirm to you that you are in harmony with the divine flow.

Trust your inner conviction, even when your logical mind or other people come up with reasons why a certain idea will not work. Many of the most extraordinary developments in Earth reality were at one time widely considered to be risky, inappropriate, or impossible. When you form a partnership with God and begin to take risks, defy conventional thinking, or attempt what scarcely seems possible, you may be amazed at the results.

An important benefit of your willingness to trust God and follow your internal guidance can be greater self-confidence. You will gain an appreciation of who you are as a soul and why you are here. This becomes a rising spiral toward even greater trust and sharing yourself in service.

We support you and are happy to share our energy and cooperation whenever you ask. We are brothers and sisters in the Light. We bless you.

> Much Love,
>
> Your Guides and Friends who are in spirit at this time
>
> Trust yourself and God. We will all succeed.

DAY 32

Living in Unity and Service

Love and Light are yours for the asking. These blessings are also offered to your loved ones. You can help yourself and others receive Divine Love and healing with a sincere request from your heart to God.

If your motives are unselfish and loving, the results will be compatible with that vibration. Purity of intention is an important way that your inner being can influence the reality you experience.

Most people do not fully realize the power to create that exists within them. Your innate creativity, when aligned with Divine Love, is a tremendous healing force, able to improve whatever is out of order in your life or in your world. The power of Love can heal every being and every difficulty on planet Earth.

Then why hasn't this healing already occurred? Because it is necessary for more people to accept this magnificent Divine energy and to radiate it to your world. It will require coordinated efforts by willing world servers to co-create the changes that are desperately needed. There is inspiring potential for changes of great magnitude to take place in Earth reality.

It is imperative for enough human beings to realize that Divine energy, which holds such wonderful potential for your planet, is a benevolent force emanating from God. Divine Grace has a continuous beneficial influence directly upon all evolving life, but Divine Love must radiate *through the hearts and actions of individuals* to have the most powerful effect in your physical dimension.

Therefore, if you wish to be part of the unfolding planetary healing, put your attention first on your own heart rather than on things outside yourself. Bring your unique talents, your full engagement, and your heartfelt motive of service to contribute in harmony with the gifts of others. Great things can be accomplished most effectively by groups of responsible individuals working in cooperation with God and each other.

In this millennium, you will find the energies of responsibility and Love expanding in your physical reality and reaching greater expression through each person. Mankind will awaken to feelings of Oneness with the entire family of life. Choosing unity will not lead to individuals melting their essences together as if they were in one big saucepot. Letting go of your personality's unhealed motives and sense of separateness will not mean that you lose your identity or individuality. Instead, your decision to join each other in unity will be more like the creation of a delicious salad. Each complementary ingredient in a salad retains its distinct taste and texture, combining them in harmony for a positive outcome. Likewise, when people collaborate on a project, the synergy of their contributions can produce a result that is greater than the sum of its parts.

Oneness brings awareness that you are part of a whole, an important element whose particular quality cannot be duplicated by any other. Each individual is meant to share their own distinct essence and specific abilities in cooperation with the diverse gifts of others. Just like the instruments in an orchestra, members of a team, organs of a body, or parts of an engine, each person has an important role. The quality of each individual's highest contribution is developed through willingness and persistence.

The diversity of world servers includes every type of person as well as other forms of life, seen and unseen, that you may have only begun to consider. Each one has a unique and needed contribution to make. Look forward to this cooperation. It will be fascinating, uplifting, and productive beyond what you have dreamed. The miraculous unfoldment of peace and harmonious sharing throughout your world can only manifest fully within an atmosphere of openness and love.

Continue opening your heart to enrich your connection with all life. Pray for Divine Love to radiate into the hearts of everyone. Love will be received in your reality and also in many other dimensions.

We bless you, dear friend. Our communion with you is loving and joyful. Ask to feel it and you will. Keep inviting the Presence of God to be active in your life.

The willingness to accept responsibility for taking steps toward healing must come from you. You always have free will. The element of free choice will make our communion even sweeter when we all choose unity with God and each other.

>Love and blessings,
>
>Your many loving Guides and Friends
>
>Your willing and open heart is the key.

DAY 33

Appreciating Your Individuality

Love is to you what water and sunshine are to a garden. Divine Love continually supports your life and nourishes your growth. You already have seeds within you containing the potential of all you can become, but to flourish, seeds require environments that are beneficial to their particular species.

All plants require a particular habitat for their health and survival. Some plants do best in acidic soil, some in alkaline. Some like to be close to their neighbors; others need more space. Many ferns develop best within the shadow and protection of taller plants, while a cactus may thrive independently in the sun. Yet all plants need light and nourishment.

We encourage you to look at the circumstances of your life and be willing to seek the surroundings that will best nurture the growth of your particular characteristics and abilities. You do not help yourself by attempting to become established in the wrong growing conditions for your needs, even if that environment seems perfect for many other people.

You have come to planet Earth to allow your truest self to blossom and bear fruit. Your presence and positive interactions are valuable contributions to the ecology here. If you have experiences that seem less than successful, they are not wasted. They can provide insight and enrichment for your next growing season when you try again.

Learn to appreciate your personal contribution and give it your best effort. Remember to also value the differences and unique contributions of others. Every individual is important.

This principle is reflected on Earth throughout nature. All species and all beings have something essential to offer and can be inspiring when we remember to appreciate them.

Love and respect for yourself are important to your spiritual growth because these attitudes help you value and develop your individuality. When you love and appreciate others, you can see their divinity and the perfection of their presence in your life and your world. In this way, you can make great progress toward understanding your Oneness with God and all life.

You have many celestial gardeners around you, lovingly helping to provide you with a fertile environment and appropriate care. Growth comes from within each individual through instinct and willingness. Like your friends in the plant kingdom, it is your inborn nature to seek the Light, to grow, and to express your unique qualities.

Bless you. Know that you are beautiful and valuable. There is no possible substitute for you. Know that you are loved beyond your comprehension.

>With unlimited devotion,
>
>Your Guides and Friends in spirit
>
>It is our joy to be of service to you and to God.

DAY 34

Brotherhood and Transformation

Wake up to the glorious experience of God's Love. Divine Love is all around you, available for you to receive and use. Each person is meant to accept Divine energy and to express it through their actions. Until enough individuals choose to participate in its transmission, the power of Divine Love cannot fully benefit your world.

A great transformation is underway. Divine Love is blessing your reality more every day and your heart wants to respond. Your soul incarnated in a physical body at this time in Earth's long history because you wanted to experience the remarkable quality of Love now encompassing the Earth. Earth desperately needs this expanding radiance of Divine Love to heal the hearts and interactions of mankind.

Through worldwide media, humanity has shared many collective experiences of grief, wonder, and greater awareness of diversity. The things you have in common have decreased your feelings of distance and detachment from each other. You are healing your illusions of insulation and invulnerability to each other's circumstances, which is leading you to recognition of brotherhood among all of humanity. This deepening understanding of your Oneness increasingly promotes connection, respect, and synergy between mankind and the many other forms of life in God's grand Creation.

There is conscious life existing within your plant and mineral kingdoms, within your planet, your galaxy, and beyond. There are also many forms of life that are not physical but are nonetheless quite real and alive. Some of us are communicating with you right now.

There are more people living on your planet than ever before in Earth's history. There are even more souls existing in other dimensions than are currently incarnated in Earth reality. Countless souls desire the opportunities in your world for personal growth and service that these momentous times offer.

Many souls living on Earth right now are seeking opportunities for leadership and contribution during this age of transformation. There are abundant opportunities to evolve through activities of service to others. Your greatest service of all could be your consistent alignment with God and sincere dedication to your personal healing, especially if you pray for God to share the benefits of similar healings wherever they are needed. Your own progress contributes to the upliftment of humanity as well as to the spiritual growth of your precious personality and soul.

These are not easy times for much of humanity. In some cases, the illusions of separateness from each other and from God are severe and may require drastic circumstances to dissolve them. Tragedy and misfortune can be catalysts for the emergence of compassion and unity when people open their hearts in a spirit of brotherhood and take action to help.

Developing willingness to change is very difficult for many egos, but the Higher Self of each person will continue to create the needed opportunities for recognizing interconnectedness. Love of self, love of others, and love of God will be a satisfying process as well as your goal. Great challenges are ahead, but wondrous improvements can be accomplished on planet Earth by flowing with the energies of Love and change rather than resisting them.

You can see clearly that faith, personal healing, and a sense of brotherhood among all people are urgently needed in your present reality. You are fortunate to have the opportunity to participate in the co-creation of these developments. The effort is challenging, but you have abundant support if you ask for it. You will also be able to carry forward a sense of accomplishment and fulfillment far into the future because of your own willing contribution in this lifetime.

Be assured that you already have the inclinations and potential that you need for your irreplaceable role in this great enterprise. Take time to attune to the impulses within your heart concerning your personal path through life. Become willing to follow your inner guidance and to develop your whole self, even if others find your path puzzling, impractical, or irrelevant. The more you follow your intuition and personal direction, the more interesting and rewarding your life becomes. You will notice the parts of your life fitting together and making more sense.

It is a privilege to be human at this time because of the plentiful opportunities for personal growth and service. It is also a demanding challenge because of the stresses and changes happening in your life. Remember, you can be healing your own consciousness as well as bringing healing to your world. Respect yourself for your willingness and worthiness to play a part in this profound transformational process.

The advancement of Earth reality will come about as more people come into full responsibility and make choices according to their Divine Guidance. Your prayers and deep desire to know God, as well as the offering of your love and skills, will facilitate the needed changes. The global transformation is blessed and you will succeed.

You are not a victim. As you planned your incarnation with the help of your Higher Self, your soul agreed to encounter certain challenging experiences to foster your long-range spiritual evolvement. Sometimes your desire to improve difficult circumstances provides motivation to connect with God and to develop new personal capabilities.

Your soul may even choose to experience tragic events for the insights and opportunities they can provide. Painful happenings can often be catalysts for everyone involved to reach a deeper sense of connection and responsibility. When you have a compassionate response to another person's pain or misfortune, acknowledge the gift they have given you. What greater gift can one soul offer to another than an opportunity to open their heart and expand their awareness of Oneness, thus accelerating their progress toward conscious union with God?

Dear friend, we offer insight, devotion, and supportive energy as you journey toward realizing your full beauty and power. We offer vibrational assistance as you deepen your understanding of yourself and become aware of your Oneness with others. It is our great joy to see you in turn offer your support and love to the family of life.

We love you and will never abandon you, whether or not you are embodied in the physical dimension. Spiritual growth and connection with others are essential keys to a joyful and fulfilling life and afterlife.

This is important to understand because you are eternal and your process of evolving is continuous.

Open your heart to receive the Great Love, for God dwells within you. God both receives and expresses through your individual presence.

>Blessings and everlasting Love to you,
>
>Your faithful Guides and Friends in spirit
>
>In caring for yourself and others, you are serving the Divine Plan.

DAY 35

THE ROLE OF DARKNESS

Divine Love is yours right now. God and those of us in spirit who are cooperating with God are continually radiating the energy of Love to you. We are in service to you and to the Divine Plan.

Unfortunately, not all living beings are attuned to God's higher purposes yet, but intentional co-creation with God is increasing in your reality as well as in other dimensions. There are still some nonphysical entities, as well as some souls in human bodies, who are angry, confused, or in great pain. They may even be deliberately malevolent in their intentions and actions. However, there is no need to fear the ones in spirit or those in human form. If there is interference with your free will, remember that stressful occurrences are manageable when you ask for God's help. Be discerning and careful to maintain your boundaries. There are no random encounters.

Understand that you are not a victim. God has designed the dynamics of the universe so that your environment reflects back to you according to the state of your consciousness and inner attitudes. Your current environment and experiences are influenced by the degree of responsibility you have taken for yourself in this life and in previous lives. Your Higher Self facilitates experiences that are appropriate for your spiritual growth and your mission in this lifetime. Certain challenges can actually be helpful by encouraging your personality to develop insights, patterns of behavior, and specific strengths that you need. As a soul, you are attempting to develop your authentic contribution and to realize loving Oneness with all life.

You and all others originated in Light, in Oneness with the Presence of God, but some souls believe the illusion that they are dark or that they need to employ the methods of darkness. They continue to choose the difficult and painful experience of darkness due to misunderstanding, stubbornness, or fear. Individuals need only to ask for Divine Light, because Light is needed to heal personal darkness. Understand that darkness is merely the absence of light; it has no power over light. Divine Light is the Presence of God, and it can immediately begin to transform every dark being or situation when invited in.

The willingness to unite with God must come from within your heart. Willingness cannot be coerced. Union with God and brotherhood with the family of life cannot be faked or forced. When these feelings are authentic within you, your sense of fulfillment is also genuine.

You are a sovereign individual; you are entitled to make personal choices and to experience the results of those choices. This dynamic ensures that your spiritual progress will keep moving forward. This is the reason it is so important to pray to live in Light, in the Presence of God. The guidance and help from God and your Spirit Guides must be requested for us to be fully supportive in your life. This is not because we must be persuaded to give this assistance, for it is our desire and joy to do so, but we hope to be invited. We are pledged to respect your free will. The Grace of God is active on behalf of every individual, but extra floodgates of bountiful Love and support are opened with your permission.

Sometimes there are circumstances when you do encounter interference with your free will. We are referring here to your conscious personality's free will, for nothing can occur within your personal reality unless your Higher Self chooses to allow it. Your experiences are opportunities for you to be in service, to build your abilities and consistency, or to heal your remaining illusions.

The many loving spiritual beings around you would never attempt interference with you. They realize that the only valid choices for growth come from within yourself. When a misguided individual interferes with someone else's free will, that behavior is a breach of Divine Law. It is seriously counterproductive to the authentic learning and progress of any soul to be interfered with or misled.

Every individual has the right under Divine Law to make their own choices and to experience the results of their choices without interference. If they are out of order, the unwanted results will provide an opportunity to notice and self-correct. This is the path to authentic growth and reunion with God. However, there are still humans and spirit entities that have not yet learned to respect the free will of others. They attempt interference of various kinds in the mistaken belief that this can bring them control, invulnerability, or power.

Look around you and observe how often interference with someone's free will is present in commonplace incidents of conflict, intimidation, sabotage, or deceit. You may also notice powerful feelings of separateness influencing more dramatic interference, such as abuse, oppression, or violence. Interference, which is forbidden under Divine Law, may occur in personal interactions or in other areas of human activity.

Keep in mind, people acting in intrusive, manipulative or aggressive ways are in some degree of anger or insecurity. They are selfishly grasping for a sense of control or invulnerability to criticism, hardship, or helplessness. In their denial of their personal disharmony, they are desperately trying to avoid painful feelings within themselves. They are not recognizing the truth.

Human beings or entities in other dimensions that interfere are not originally evil; they merely exist in some degree of darkness. They are children of God who are at a point in their learning process where they have not yet realized that peace does not come through achieving invulnerability or control, but rather through self-respect and sharing love. Their isolation, unhappiness, and desperation increase as long as they hold on to their attitudes and allow their wounds and misbehaviors to remain unhealed. The Higher Selves of those affected by darkness may allow discomfort to intensify in the hope that these individuals, in bodies or in spirit, will develop a willingness to choose a different path. Their solution is to reach directly to God.

Darkness may serve as a catalyst, providing you with an opportunity to develop compassion or motivation to work toward change. If you feel vulnerable to some kind of interference with your free will, understand that the interference cannot take place unless you have a related vibration *within yourself* that needs healing or development. Come into full self-responsibility with this recognition. Encountering darkness or distortion in your life may bring to your attention that you have a related distortion that needs healing, especially if you experience a judgmental or upsetting emotional reaction.

Another possibility is that you have a spiritual need to interact with that darkness in order to expand your insight, skill, or sensitivity. It may also be an opportunity to develop compassion or to be in service as a healer. God may be prompting you to interact with that dark consciousness as a healing, to share Divine energy and spiritual understanding. This can only be done through prayer and partnership with God. Assisting the return of dark entities to the Light brings healing to them and to humanity.

As you progress in your understanding of darkness, you can make a daily request to live in the Light of God's Love and protection. Seek your own perfect pattern in this lifetime. Ask to be guided along the path of your greatest spiritual development, healing, and service. You can also lovingly request that this support be offered to the many beings around you in bodies and in spirit who are in need. Your prayers are a valuable way to be in service to the Divine Plan while you are healing and improving yourself. It is blessed.

The dynamics between Light and darkness are part of God's design for our universe. The dark influences are allowed to persist because they push individuals to make better decisions, to initiate connection with God, and to act more responsibly.

When human beings or individuals in any dimension experience the effects of dark sabotage or misbehavior, they usually find it objectionable or even intolerable. This can spur them to take positive action that they might otherwise neglect. Experiencing the unpleasantness of darkness may counteract inertia.

There are many problems to solve and improvements to make in your reality and in your own consciousness. If support, ease, and compassion do not prompt sufficient action, then discomfort may be needed to provide a push.

The Earth plane of existence is a school for spiritual growth and development of contributions. It is not a vacation destination. Connect with the Divine and seek to discover and fulfill the potential of your soul while you are here.

We bless you and love you. God's guidance and power are available to everyone. The goal of your life on Earth is your personal healing, expansion, and service, as you learn to become a co-creator with the Divine.

We wish you peace, Love, and Light. Every darkness and wound can be healed with perseverance and God's help. There is no absolute evil, but there can be intensely difficult learning about separation from self, from other beings, or from God. There is no need for God's forgiveness, because God does not judge you or anyone else. God has deep compassion and patient allowance for every being when their learning process becomes painful. God always loves you dearly.

If you feel judged, the judgment is coming from within yourself, not from God or your Guides. If you feel condemnation from those around you, recognize that this is a reflection of your need to fully love and forgive yourself. Taking responsibility to set things right in a situation can help you let go of self-judgment as you heal.

Understand that you are not a victim. No matter what upsetting or traumatic experiences may have taken place in your life or in the lives of those you know, every soul involved has attracted those experiences according to their own spiritual needs for perspective, self-development, or new personal decisions. Sometimes the learning gained from a difficult experience provides a foundation for helping others or a basis for the soul's mission of a specific kind of service.

Reflect on the experiences in your life to discover how this point of view might be true. How could your challenging experiences in this lifetime have been constructive? Have they led to willingness to seek healing or contributed to your personal development? Have you grown in appreciation, compassion, or connection with life around you? Certain challenges may intensify in your life, contributing to your readiness to make new choices or to take action toward change. Remember, it is not *the sooner the better* regarding your best choices, it is *the sooner the easier*.

There is an interesting dynamic often apparent in progressively stressful situations such as escalating conflict or deteriorating conditions. Your struggles tend to intensify until you become willing to ask for the help you need and make constructive changes. Consistent prayer and receptivity to your Divine Guidance are important for meeting challenges most effectively. Awareness is not enough. Integration of new learning and healing into your personal attitudes and behavior is essential for your progress.

It can be very beneficial to ask for support from other people. You are designed to need each other. These connections bring increased opportunities for building intimacy, community, self-esteem, and of course, realizations of Oneness.

You are part of all life and part of God. God can express and receive expression through you. You are loved and treasured; you are also eternal. There is no final death, but there will be transition to new realities and different opportunities for your spiritual expansion and contribution. You are not going to run out of time. *The Divine purpose behind the elaborate dynamics at work in your physical reality is to support the spiritual evolvement of all individuals.*

The hard work of spiritual advancement can also be joyful and amazing. You will have renewed awareness of the Love and connection that are your birthright as your planet progresses during this millennium. The needed evolution is happening as Divine Grace responds to mankind's deepening commitment to healing, bonding, and peace. Profound improvements in your world are coming about as human beings learn to co-create the changes in partnership with God.

We bless you and join with you in love and solidarity. We are always on call. We seek to join with you in active service to humanity and all Creation.

> We will succeed!
> Your steadfast Guides and Friends in spirit
> Planet Earth is evolving along with us.

DAY 36

The Coming Era

Sense the incredible energy of Divine Love that is part of you, always present within you and around you. We are all composed of the vibrant energy of Love; it is the substance of Creation. God's Love is the catalyst for the continual evolvement of life. Remember that the purpose of the Divine Plan is to support our spiritual progress. Open your awareness and your body to Light, the Presence of God and Divine Love.

Those of us who serve as your Spirit Guides are also part of the energy of Love. We do not feel separate from each other or from those of you in human bodies. We are all One. As your team of support, we hope to help you realize this truth. Every one of us is part of God and God is part of everyone and everything in Creation. The truth of our Oneness is comforting to contemplate and it is becoming increasingly apparent in your reality.

As Earth is transitioning to the coming era, the hearts of mankind are becoming ever more receptive to the energy of God's Love. Human beings regularly invoke the Presence, the power, and the benevolence of

God. Your hearts are repeatedly opening to receiving and radiating Divine Love. The flow is expanding as you take the initiative to connect with God and express Love.

Love is taking many forms as you co-create the new era on Earth. There is supportive love within families and communities of all kinds. Selfless love is increasingly motivating the work of individuals and of organizations. Love for humanity is becoming an important component of education, health care, science, government, the arts, and private enterprise.

Mankind is becoming increasingly successful as selfless service, communication, and cooperation enhance the important contributions that individuals are making. Altruism and collaboration are the foundation of your progress toward innovation, vibrant health, productivity, and brotherhood on Earth. The dynamic energy of Divine Love is always available to encourage and amplify these developments, but willingness to make an effort must emerge from individual hearts.

At the present time in humanity's evolvement, some people are attempting to make a contribution to the world from motives of selfish gain rather than service. Some misguided individuals attempt to develop their gifts without sharing. Because physical reality reflects back to a person according to the state of their consciousness, these individuals may find their projects collapsing or failing to ripen, even when the seeds seemed quite promising.

There is an explanation for this undesired outcome: a person's intentions and degree of alignment with the Divine Plan influence their results. An individual soul is still learning and attempting to heal feelings of insecurity and separateness while seeking their return to conscious unity with God. Their Higher Self, in Oneness with God, repeatedly offers needed experiences and insights to support this progress. The Higher Self hopes the human personality will choose to live in peace and to act with the intention of service. Your Higher Consciousness tirelessly constructs circumstances and feedback to encourage your nobility.

Be in integrity with the Divine energy flowing through you. Be consistently receptive and responsive to God. You can be a co-creator with God as your partner. Nurture and value your creative contribution, whatever it may be. Stay willing and ready to express yourself and to serve. Mutual appreciation and collaboration with others are leading to pivotal new developments and harmony in the coming era on Earth.

Productive and exhilarating times are ahead. As you achieve more peace, wholeness, and forward momentum, these factors are becoming more apparent in your external environment as well. It is blessed and meant to be.

Each individual affects all others; we impact all experience and all evolvement. None of us is completely successful until we are all successful. However, the genuine willingness to assume responsibility for your personal growth and sacred service must come from within your own heart, not from outside interference or pressure. Your Higher Self is your faithful guide toward willingness, whether you are in a body or between lifetimes. Your soul and the various personalities of your many incarnations need each other in order to make this progress.

We can offer each other love and companionship as those of us in bodies and in spirit journey together in pursuit of expansion and service. We can also have fun together as we learn from each other and co-create with God.

May God bless you and keep you. We love you.

Your Guides and Friends in spirit

The realization of Oneness is joyous!

DAY 37

Receptivity and Responsiveness to Guidance

Love is the foundation for mankind's greatest accomplishments. When you conceive a project with sincere motives of contribution and unselfish service, your next step is to align your personal will with the Will of God. As your creativity is elevated to intentional co-creation with God by your practices of receptivity and responsiveness to your Divine Guidance, you receive even more inspiration and support.

There may be some surprising developments or unexpected timing, but noble motives plus actions aligned with the Will of God ultimately yield positive results. This sequence allows you to contribute effectively to the Divine Plan for Creation.

Search your own heart. If the motives you find there do not enhance your self-respect and inner peace, realize that you can change them. Be willing to revise your intentions and actions; this alters the nature of what is being reflected back to you by your surroundings and companions. Acknowledge your willingness to change, then ask God for the guidance and help you need.

It is helpful to declare your desire to change in a physical way, either spoken aloud or expressed on paper. This makes your new decision very clear to your Higher Self and the Guides around you. They will immediately do all they can to support and inspire you.

If you are alert, you will notice synchronicities that bring information and encouragement for your new path. There may also be important opportunities to say no to certain directions. Go within, seeking to know God's Will through prayer and receptivity, and attune to your heartfelt instincts about your next steps. Your spiritual practice helps you clarify the pathway forward that supports your highest motivations and goals.

Each person is unique; what is best for one may cause delay or even damage to another. As a human being, you are the final authority for your personal life choices because you have free will. Even so, your Higher Consciousness has a much wider and truer perspective regarding your decisions than your humanity does. Your conscious personality experiences the most productive and satisfying results when you are continually receptive and responsive to the guidance from your Higher Self and God.

Your Higher Self knows that you are part of God

and that God is part of you. Your Higher Self stays in touch with your soul's intentions for this incarnation. Deep within your heart, your highest hopes for your own possibilities are the same as God's.

However, your human personality might be unduly influenced by people, advice, or pressures around you. If you do not reach to God, you may overlook your most valuable source of guidance and support. When making decisions, consider your deepest feelings, your attractions and aversions, and the synchronicities that have occurred. Information and advice can be useful, but we encourage you to examine your true feelings when determining the personal relevance of any information or opinion.

As you are learning to recognize your intuition and heartfelt inclinations as Divine Guidance, it is necessary to distinguish these from any unhealed impulses or reactions of your ego. Examine deeply and honestly your motivation behind an urge to speak or act. Be honest with yourself if your motive for any action is manipulation, selfish gain, or attainment of status. If you are seeking validation or invulnerability, then your personality's priorities are in control.

Adjust your intentions to be in total integrity with God and to heal and develop yourself with a goal of service. You can trust your inner guidance when it is compatible with these noble aspirations. If your intuition promotes a desire for wisdom and understanding or for loving interaction with life around you, then you are receiving guidance and encouragement from your Higher Self.

Become willing to comply with your Divine Guidance. Allow yourself to trust and follow your positive instincts. When you are truly connected with God and the deepest part of yourself, then hesitation and prolonged analysis are counterproductive.

Practice flowing with the momentum of your inner guidance, rather than resisting it. Life always involves challenges, but your receptivity to God and willingness to take action lead you more efficiently to accomplishment, fulfillment, and joy. The path of resistance creates a detour delaying your progress. Either way, you will be provided with new opportunities to master the learning and evolvement your soul is hoping to attain. Divine Guidance is always available to you as you make new decisions. God will support you.

We abide with you, whatever your choices. We seek to serve you and God's evolving Creation. We hope for your invitation to collaborate.

>God bless you.
>
>Your loving Guides and Friends in spirit
>
>There is no failure, no time limit, no wrath of God. You are learning.

DAY 38

CO-CREATION AND THE DIVINE PLAN

Love is leading to a glorious renaissance of mankind. A great awakening is taking place on planet Earth. It is happening in the hearts and minds of humanity as Divine Love enhances all areas of your civilization. The expanding renaissance is a healing and spiritual renewal for your entire world.

Physical and spiritual healing are both needed on Earth right now. Your planetary environment has become dangerously polluted with hazardous substances and contamination in the ground, waters, and air. Unfortunately, there are also feelings of unworthiness, fear, and anger in the hearts and minds of many people.

This situation cannot continue. It is imperative that you improve the ecology of your planet before conditions deteriorate further. Healing is desperately needed in your physical and spiritual environments for Earth to flourish as the beautiful and uplifting place of exploration and expression that it is meant to be. The healing of Earth is planned and blessed by God. It is happening as a result of the prayers and co-creative efforts of humanity.

Great changes are taking place in your planetary reality; they are challenging but necessary. The crises are planned to motivate individuals to form an intentional partnership with God. God has also designed certain events to encourage compassion and acts of generosity. Supportive cooperation is strengthening your bonds with each other and accelerating your planet's transformation. The healing of your world is destined to come about because the universe will eternally support it, but the timing is affected by your free will choices and actions. The need is urgent for individuals to become more responsible.

Give thought to current news events and trends. Consider situations in your own experience and in the lives of others. Notice how certain circumstances highlight areas of needed healing and problem solving. As mankind accomplishes the necessary developments, you will notice worldwide shifts ushering in a welcome New Age of infinite positive outcomes for humanity.

The individual and planetary crises happening now are actually opportunities for growth. The challenges have been consented to by the Higher Self of every being who is affected. The willingness to cooperate with God to accomplish your learning and develop your service must come from within your own heart. You always have free will. As you respond to conditions and events, you are choosing your attitudes and actions.

The changes and challenges in your world are occurring because of the immense and tender Love that God has for every being in Creation. The difficulties are not evidence of divine wrath or punishment. No one is being judged as a sinner or wrongdoer. With limitless empathy and patience, God recognizes humanity's profound need for healing and for greater awareness of Divine Love. God is offering these blessings to you. If you accept, you will feel the Love and support.

The spiritual part of yourself has chosen every lifetime you have experienced. You have come into a physical body for a purpose. With guidance from your Higher Self, your soul has planned your companions, your circumstances, and the influences upon you in every incarnation. Your environment reflects the state of your consciousness to you so that you are constantly creating the lessons you need. The choices made by your human personality merely affect the specific situations and timing of your scheduled learning. It is not the sooner the better that you accomplish your goals, but you will find that sooner is easier.

There is no need to fear the challenges and lessons ahead. Instead, look forward to increased awareness of Love and Light surrounding you and your world.

Lovingly focus on your rituals of prayer, receptivity, and honoring the Divine. Develop your willingness to respond promptly and completely to the voice within you, the intuitive guidance resulting from your alignment and personal walk with God. Life on Earth is meant to be joyful and fulfilling; your devotion and persistence will help to bring this about.

Have loving allowance for yourself as you practice your co-creative approach to life and spiritual growth. Your ego may have some resistance to change or reluctance to let go of control. Your inner child, the emotional aspect of your personality, may have an objection or reaction that you feel as intense emotion. These responses will subside as you observe that things are improving. Your trust in God, altruistic intentions, and willingness to act will increase as you repeatedly notice that your co-creative approach is effective.

Pray for the help that is important for yourself, for others, and for conditions on your planet. There is powerful assistance available from God and the many helpful beings around you in physical bodies and in spirit. Abundant support comes in answer to your heartfelt prayers. Improvements occur as you become willing to express your gifts and serve others with genuine love and generosity. Mankind's pursuit of healing through prayer and responsible action has already made a difference. Humanity's spiritual progress has already reduced the need for some of the serious challenges that could have been necessary to focus humanity's attention and open the way for the new era. God continually updates the Divine Plan, taking into consideration all internal and external factors affecting each new moment.

You will be successful, individually and collectively. You are now involved in a dramatic transformation of consciousness on your planet. There will be a continuing expansion of Love, cooperation, and peace in your world. You will become increasingly sensitive to the Divine Presence within your heart and within others. People are realizing that we all belong to the family of God. This remarkable progress is a manifestation of the Divine Plan. It is blessed.

You are more precious than you know. Believe that you are needed and important. Every individual has an effect on all others and on the entire universe. We are all connected and each of us has a spiritual mission. We continuously draw to ourselves the divine response to our current spiritual needs and goals.

We are all creating through the genuine attitudes in our hearts, as well as through all our choices and actions. When we align our personal will with Divine Will, God coordinates the Divine Plan with grace and ease. Let each of us humbly and faithfully practice co-creation in partnership with God.

God bless you. We are always nearby.
Your Guides and Friends in spirit
We are allies in a great cause.

DAY 39

The Purpose of Individuation

Love is a natural and extraordinary gift of mankind. As the transformation of beautiful planet Earth accelerates, all life is becoming more aware of humanity's inspiring capacity for love. Many people already recognize in themselves and others genuine compassion, generosity, and desire for connection. These beautiful qualities are your greatest strengths as human beings. Your love is your gift to yourselves and to the rest of Creation.

When you allow Divine Love into your heart and are willing to share it with others, you are offering a priceless service to your world. You are contributing to saving your planet. Your prayers for peace and brotherhood as well as for the end of dysfunction, greed, and violence are certainly helping to co-create better conditions in your reality. The energies of prayers are cumulative; your repeated invocations are important. A tremendous number of people are expressing their free will through their prayers and behavior and that collective choice has set in motion the ordained healing of planet Earth.

At first, Divine Love expands in your heart, encouraging you to join with others as you express Love in the values and efforts of your communities and nations. Abundant loving support is available, but individuals must be the *initiators* of healing in your world through personal responsibility and Love in action. This is how you demonstrate to God your spiritual maturity and readiness for the planetary healing you seek.

A new era is already dawning. It has been planned and anticipated for centuries. Your planet has begun a vibrational readjustment that will support individuals with their willingness to rely on God.

Many people could do severe spiritual harm to themselves if they choose to continue on their present pathways of selfishness, addiction, dishonesty, or violence. They would be descending deeper into the illusion of separation. With great patience and Love, the Higher Self of each person continues to provide conditions designed to encourage willingness to change. These circumstances are opportunities to put the purposes of the soul ahead of the limited and temporary priorities of the human personality. Every soul's spiritual purpose is learning to co-create with God in order to make valuable contributions to the family of life.

Sometimes an individual refuses the learning and healing opportunities offered throughout their lifetime, allowing their personal distortions and pain to intensify. At some point, that soul may be called home to the Light before more serious spiritual damage is done. The individual soul will not be judged, but instead will be received with compassion and offers of healing for their present condition. The individual will be offered Love and new perspectives during the interval between incarnations. When the soul feels ready, the Higher Self and the soul will then plan for the next lifetime with the help of God and their loving Guides. They will schedule new opportunities for the soul to develop the needed personal responsibility, receptivity to God, and loving heart. Consciousness is eternal and no one will run out of time to return to God.

Our personal needs for growth and understanding influence our next learning priorities. Each of us experiences the consequences of our thoughts and actions sooner or later. We are the creators of our reality, never the victims. Every individual we encounter is a creator as well, not a victim of anyone else.

During an incarnation, an individual's Higher Self may allow difficult circumstances or events to help that person develop their willingness to seek truth, to heal, and to ask for needed assistance. Our Higher Selves live in Oneness, working cooperatively with God for our spiritual benefit. Our Higher Selves provide guidance and arrange the situations that we need for our spiritual progress and the development of our service.

Unpleasant conditions during a lifetime may be agreed to by souls before their birth. They hope the difficulties will serve as catalysts for their spiritual growth. Life challenges may be selected in advance as a way of gaining specific understanding, making a particular contribution, or encouraging the personality to accept responsibility as a creator. Souls are both growing and healing as they journey through multiple lifetimes.

In spirit, the reflection of a soul's intention and state of consciousness is instantaneous. In the physical dimension a human personality has the impression of sequential time. In your reality things seem to happen more slowly and in sequence or stages. This can help you notice the relationship between cause and effect.

When necessary, the trials and limitations experienced in the physical dimension can cause someone to feel dissatisfaction with any disharmony they are creating. Unease may intensify until a person develops willingness to change and determination to do whatever it takes to create a more constructive and harmonious experience. The changes occur in an individual's heart before they manifest in their outer reality, which always reflects the vibration needed by their consciousness.

We hope you do not use this concept of reflection as a basis for self-criticism when things do not seem to be going well. The feedback you gain from your surroundings and experiences can motivate new decisions about going forward. If you were creating perfectly, you would have no need to be human. We encourage you to acknowledge yourself instead for accepting the challenge of healing your illusions of unworthiness or separateness. We hope you will practice your creatorship with integrity and nobility. Pray for the Love and help you need. They are your birthright as a child of God, no matter what you have or have not done.

As you do the spiritual work of healing any unease you feel within yourself, you are in service to God and all mankind. The Grace of God will support you. As you heal a specific aspect of disharmony within your own consciousness, you also improve that specific vibration in the wider reality. Those who have a personal connection with a dysfunction are in a position to contribute most effectively to its widespread healing. They can understand the aspects of the issue and have empathy for the suffering involved. A non-judgmental heart is the best conduit for divine healing energy.

You may have noticed an absence of peace in your own reactions and behavior. You may be concerned about how a difficulty is showing up in your personal life or in your world. As you recognize that an attitude or pattern of behavior is out of order, you can accept the responsibility and challenge of taking the steps needed to bring healing. The blessing of the healing energy comes from God in Divine right timing, but the role of an individual is also important. Your commitment to incarnate on your planet gives you the right to invoke healing for humanity. You have a physical connection with Earth and you can contribute to life in your dimension in ways that require human attributes. Divine healing is invoked when a person recognizes the need and makes a prayer request for help.

Your role in your own healing involves acknowledging your need, resolving to make changes, asking for qualified help, and creating occasions for healing to take place. If Angels could complete the healing for you, it would already be done, but that would not empower you or support your development as a co-creator with God. This system, which requires sincerity and self-responsibility, ensures that your progress is authentic. It is God's careful design for planet Earth school.

When you pray for another person or situation, be willing to personally serve the healing. You can offer to be a physical conduit for Divine energy to flow through you to address what is needed. Anyone who is willing can invoke and radiate Divine energy. The more you purify your own energy field by personal work on yourself and continue to practice being a channel for the Divine, the more you increase your intuition and your capacity to transmit blessings to your dimension and beyond.

You can release every healing into the care of God, asking that it be thorough and ongoing until it is complete in God's sight. Work big. Ask for the blessings of similar healings to be shared throughout Creation wherever the current Will of God directs. Your invocation, participation, and request for God to distribute healing are a valuable and sacred service.

The healing of painful personal and societal difficulties in your planetary environment can be done *with you*, but not for you. The problems stem from the anxiety and defenses that souls develop as a result of experiencing the illusion that they are separate from God. This uncomfortable predicament is not due to any failure or fall from Grace. Experiencing the stressful feeling of separateness is an unavoidable side effect of your individuation. When you individuate, you temporarily forget the truth of your Oneness with all life and you experience yourself as a separate individual. Many misunderstandings, misbehaviors, and defenses can develop from the resulting feelings of insecurity and your attempts to cope or compensate.

Remember, there is a Divine purpose behind the process and perils of individuation. For you to work your way through all the troubles you will encounter, it is important to develop a practice of repeatedly connecting with God and responding to your internal guidance. As you learn to heal the counterproductive attitudes and behaviors resulting from the stress of experiencing yourself as a separate individual, you are *simultaneously* developing the specific spiritual practices and capacities needed by an effective co-creator with God. This is the wisdom of God supporting your ongoing progress.

The higher purpose of your struggles is to provide motivation and opportunities to refine your personal qualities and strength of character. You grow spiritually as you do the necessary work to overcome the challenges you encounter. You are a co-creator in training. The extraordinary potential for learning to co-create with God is the reason you chose to take on the illusion of separateness. In Oneness, before you individuated, the deep desire of your Higher Consciousness was to contribute something new and needed to Creation. Your aspiration to be of service is the foundation of your courage and resilience as you move through your series of lifetimes.

While you are in the physical dimension exploring the experience of individuality and developing self-responsibility, it is helpful to understand the dynamics of Light and darkness and their relationship to your growth as a soul. Light and darkness have often been regarded as opposites that are in conflict with each other. Most of humanity now experiences the forces of duality as if they are competing influences of good and evil. The paradox is that they are actually designed by God as *complementary* forces that work *in combination* to help you clarify your choices and intentions. Together they motivate your spiritual progress. The darkness pushes you with discomfort, prodding you to reconsider and act. The Light inspires and attracts you. Both polarities support you as you move forward toward full recognition of your Oneness with everything.

The Grace of God continually helps you on your journey. The Love and assistance from God and many servers of the Light are always available. With Divine support, you can achieve your spiritual mastery. You can bring healing to yourself and your reality, becoming an effective co-creator of the future.

Focus on discovering and honoring the beauty within you; remember to love yourself. Self-esteem is not arrogant or counterproductive. Arrogance is a defensive quality of separateness and a closed heart. Arrogance is an attempt to compensate for feelings of insufficiency or unworthiness. On the other hand, self-esteem is a feeling of wholeness that develops within you as you recognize that you are repeatedly *giving your best effort with your best intentions*. Loving your true self and appreciating all that you are willing to give enables you to keep your heart open with those around you. This is how you create healing, progress, and peace in your world.

We are meant to love and help each other, for we are all One. Your aspiration is to heal and develop yourself so you can generously serve the family of life. When you respect yourself, you feel deserving of the Divine Love that is continuously surrounding you, available to be invited and allowed in. Say yes to God.

Each of us in every dimension and every reality is loved and cherished, without exception. As your Spirit Guides, our deep desire is to help create an environment on planet Earth where the truth that you belong to God's family is easy to feel and understand. The certainty that you are loved is going to become joyfully apparent in your world from infancy through the transition back to spirit. This will become a strong foundation supporting you as you evolve and express yourself in every lifetime.

A new era on Earth is beginning and with God's help we will co-create it together. We will enjoy the transformation, sharing love as we celebrate the wonder of it. May God bless us all as we choose unity and make our contributions to the Divine Plan.

> We join with you in this great adventure!
> Your dedicated Guides and Friends in spirit
> We will always love you.

DAY 40

THE BLESSINGS OF DIVINE LOVE

Love is in your environment already. Sacred energy surrounds you. As you open your heart inviting in Divine Love, you expand your personal capacity to bring blessings into your consciousness and your world.

Allowing the energy of Divine Love to flow through your heart has valuable benefits. Love can enrich feelings of solidarity and harmony in human interactions on every level. The presence of Love also supports your physical and emotional health. This is now becoming more apparent throughout your civilization.

We would like to emphasize that giving Love and care is even more beneficial spiritually than receiving them. Lovingly expressing your wisdom, skills, and friendship leads to your own greatest expansion. As you connect with the power of God's Love, sharing that Love through your open heart, the outward flow allows you to draw even more Divine energy into yourself. It is continuously replenished because the Source of this energy is unlimited.

Transmitting Divine energy is more sustainable than sharing from your personal energy because personal energy can become depleted while Source energy is infinite. Working in partnership with God multiplies your own potential for sharing healing and support. This is the remarkable synergy of co-creation.

Loving yourself is also a valuable component of your spiritual service. Healthy self-esteem is needed to attain your greatest success and connection with others. It is not just okay to appreciate yourself and your gifts, it is vitally important. As you build consistency in your relationship with God, allow your growing confidence to inspire gratitude within you. Let gratitude nourish your heart and your desire to serve.

Divine Love alive within you also enhances your personal creativity. The true motives in your heart have a powerful effect on your contribution. Listening to your inner voice and appreciating the love you give yourself and others can lead to your greatest healing and service. Developing and expressing yourself with the intention of uplifting others and humanity as a whole ultimately leads to beneficial results, although sometimes in unexpected ways.

The value of sacred intent applies to every area of life on Earth, not just the ones that are obviously altruistic or innovative. Working in partnership with God and maintaining dedicated intention to develop your skills and sensitivity will lead to your most satisfying achievements. You can become your best self.

Co-creation can enrich every personal or professional pursuit. Sacred service is important to keep in mind when caring for life and situations around you. Your noble intentions help you create supportive environments and conditions of cooperation. Adopting the motives of love and unselfish service leads to greater insight and accomplishment in every field of endeavor. All beings and all talents are essential for the great work ahead.

Consider the concept of success. Your success might not include awards, fame, or wealth. Your Higher Self influences the amount of material abundance in your life in order to facilitate the lessons and contributions your soul has chosen to focus on in this incarnation.

You do have the potential to achieve a successful spiritual unfoldment in each lifetime. You are meant to develop the abilities and gifts that are already within you, available to be nurtured and expanded. You deserve to have a sense of security and well-being. You are worthy of love from your physical and your celestial companions. You have the capacity to keep your heart open, continually receiving and expressing God's Love. Whatever your age, occupation, or limitations, you can pray and invoke Divine blessings for life around you.

To thrive as you live your life, rely on prayers, intuition, and action. Spiritual practices can guide you step-by-step on your path to success. It is useful to request God's help, asking without attachment to a specific result. Quiet processes of receptivity to the sacred voice within you, along with sincere willingness to respond promptly, support your direction and momentum. The repeated sequence of prayer, receptivity to guidance, and responsive action is the miraculous process of an individual co-creating with God.

God blesses your life and supports your progress. You will know you are successful, not when others praise you or pay you well, but when you feel it in your heart. Until you feel peace within your heart, you will not really believe it if others say you are successful. If your heart already feels loving, deserving, and on your best path, what others say in the moment will not seem important.

Validate your special qualities and individual direction with deep honoring and inner confidence, not as a defensive reaction to others. Appreciate the exquisite generosity and pure intentions that are part of you. Pray for help to bring them forward. Know that your talents, your lessons, and even your limitations are needed and appropriate or you would not have chosen them for this lifetime.

God bless you and keep you. As you share love and healing with Mother Earth and life around you, your planet reciprocates by caring for your humanity. As the

Earth increases her support for you in gratitude for your openhearted service here, your life can become more abundant and secure. Those of us beyond your physical dimension also love and support you. We pray for you. We relay the radiance of Divine spiritual nourishment and protection toward you. We applaud and cheer as you flourish and interact in a spirit of Oneness.

>Receive our Love and honoring.
>
>Your many Guardians and Friends in spirit
>
>Every one of us has the potential to
>co-create with God.

DAY 41

Accepting Responsibility

Divine Love is always ready to support you. Open yourself to be continually ready to receive Love. Allow peace, wonder, and nourishing Divine energy into your heart. Remember you are cherished and blessed.

The facilitation and inspiration from your Higher Self can draw you forward through life like a boat pulls a water skier on the water. If you rely on God's support, you can experience more power and buoyancy in your process of enjoying and contributing to life.

Imagine someone learning to water ski. A beginning water skier starts out floating behind a boat and holding on to a towrope. As the boat begins to move forward, the front tip of the ski must be kept above the surface of the water. As the skier leans back, the boat's increasing speed pulls his whole body up out of the water with the ski under him. With the skier holding the rope, the forward momentum keeps him up on the surface.

Learning to relax and let go of control may seem difficult at first. When an inexperienced skier's arms and body are tense with resistance to the towrope, he can easily become tired and sore. He may lose his balance and find himself unexpectedly splashing back into the water. Then he can receive some coaching and encouragement to try again.

When the water skier learns through practice to lean back, relax, and allow the boat to pull him along, he finds himself riding on top of the water instead of plowing through it. The ride becomes less stressful and more fun as the skier begins to trust the new process. He discovers that persistence and cooperation with the forward movement produce the best results.

The driver of the boat steers, while the skier rides along behind the boat and learns to enjoy the fun and challenge of mastering the waves in his path. The boat driver navigates, while the skier concerns himself with what is immediately in front of him. As his skills and conditioning improve, the water skier becomes ready and eager for greater challenges and greater exhilaration. He can even appreciate the scenery, master some advanced maneuvers, and wave to other skiers as he rides easily on top of the water. Water skiing still requires effort, but with practice it becomes a joy instead of a struggle.

Your Higher Self is the driver of your boat. Your Higher Self knows the best direction for your life. As a soul, you made decisions about your lessons and goals before you entered into your physical body to accomplish them. Even now, you frequently consult in the dream state with your Higher Self and the Higher Consciousness of others you interact with. You are a creator. Realize that nothing is accidental and nothing is hopeless. You can choose to be on a positive path of growth and evolution toward remembrance of your Oneness with all life.

For you to attain the deep inner peace of recognizing Oneness, it is necessary for you to dissolve your illusions of separateness from other people and other life experiences. You also need to fully understand that you are an eternal Divine being who is the creator of your own experience. Take responsibility for your creatorship.

Be very clear that this does not mean blaming yourself for what you have created. It means accepting responsibility for accomplishing the healing and learning that are specific to your life plan. As a responsible creator, you realize that your own intentions, attitudes, and actions are continually contributing to your experience of reality.

Becoming consciously responsible for your life involves compassionately acknowledging yourself for your willingness to attempt your learning, no matter how difficult. Appreciate the Divine brilliance within yourself that has generated the perfect situations for you to learn, develop, and heal in the ways that have led to exactly what you have accomplished so far. These circumstances were created for your greatest growth, even though they may have seemed very challenging or distressing at the time.

Some scenarios highlight or intensify a difficult issue to help your ego become willing to keep your heart open, to ask for help, or to take constructive action. Do not criticize yourself or others when things are not going well from your personality's viewpoint. Acknowledge your need to change behavior, get creative, or shift your approach to a problem; then ask for assistance. It may be important to take personal action or to speak up in a particular situation. You may need to dig deep within yourself to find patience, unconditional love, or a path to personal healing.

Accomplishing change involves prayer, of course, and often includes asking a qualified person for help. God does not intend for you to proceed on your path of learning by yourself. We are all connected and designed to need each other. We are part of each other and part of God; no individual is fully successful until we all succeed. Unity is your destiny. No one will be left out.

You are eternal; therefore, you will not run out of time. Keep practicing. You will reach a level of mastery that enables you to struggle less and get more enjoyment from your process of learning and self-expression, just as the water skier does while skimming happily upon the surface of the water.

Every person has their own style and their own potential contribution. Creation will be beautiful as these contributions are all developed and willingly joined together. Remaining open and honestly evaluating your progress as you go helps you make good decisions. Repeated self-correction greatly accelerates your continuing evolvement.

When you conclude a physical lifetime and return to your natural nonphysical state of consciousness, you will review all the events and experiences of that completed incarnation. By examining your life, you can gain a deeper understanding of the spiritual progress you have made. You can then evaluate your needs and hopes for additional growth. As you consider your life experiences from your soul's perspective, your own sense of fulfillment or regret is the only consequence you face.

No one in spirit is judging you. When you return to the Light, joyful reunions await. You will be welcomed with Love and acceptance. You will be offered comfort and companionship. Just as you have free will when you are in a body, in spirit it will be your choice whether to allow Love to be your foundation.

Your personal healing and expansion can be increased by repeatedly evaluating your progress throughout your life. This gives you the option to self-correct because you will have many opportunities to adjust your attitudes and behavior. Honest self-examination facilitates more spiritual unfoldment within a single incarnation.

Attend to your practices of connection with your Higher Self and God. Pray for help and clarification; notice the understanding that comes to you from your intuition and clues in your environment. Your insight is an indication of your inner creatorship. Your receptivity leads to joy and satisfaction as you develop and contribute in co-creation with God.

We bless you, dear friend. We are always nearby with Love and support. When you call on God, we often respond also with God's permission. There are many of us in other dimensions who are in dedicated service to God. We strive to serve you and all Creation, for we are all One.

> In Love and Unity,
>
> Your Guides and Friends in spirit
>
> We are your unseen family.

DAY 42

Personal and Planetary Transformation

Love answers every call. Divine Love is always nearby, with you and within you. To reach the highest potential in your relationship with God, it is important for you to initiate your personal connection and express your free will; invite God to influence your life and the progress of your spiritual growth. God is hoping for a sincere invitation from you.

God has no wish to manipulate or coerce you because a true joining of hearts can take place only with the permission of every being involved. This is why unity is so precious, joyous, and reassuring, for it is freely chosen and willingly shared by all who participate. Everyone is welcome. Every individual who declines opportunities to welcome Divine Love is missed until they choose to initiate their connection. God is steadfast and patient, knowing that our eventual destiny is to unite our hearts in Love.

A widespread recognition of the Oneness of all life is now approaching. The influences of God's Love are becoming more apparent among the population and cultures of planet Earth. There is more willingness here than ever before to accept and appreciate diversity. Even though we are all part of Oneness, every person needs freedom and support to follow their own instincts and to develop in their own way. Each unique individual has a contribution to make to us all, which is valuable no matter how unusual it is.

Notice how humanity is embracing the feeling of Oneness. People are becoming more willing to empathize with the difficult circumstances of others and to work on improving conditions for all. People are less likely to seek refuge in the illusion that they are somehow immune or separate from painful wounds or stressful situations themselves. This empathy is so beautiful; it demonstrates true brotherhood.

Compassion enriches our feelings of Oneness. When compassion leads to action, the person who offers help or comfort is also a beneficiary. The giver of compassion also receives a gift, the one who extends healing is healed in turn, and the one who offers love is blessed by love. Those who accept acts of kindness give as they receive by offering the opportunity for generosity, self-respect, and heart opening in the giver's life. This leads to greater sensitivity and bonding for all. Who can say which participant has given the grander gift?

The realization of Divine Oneness has two important aspects. First is the awareness that God and all the many different beings and events in Creation are part of you. Second, and just as important, is the realization that you are part of God and Creation as well, a very valuable part. You belong; you are essential. Creation would not be complete without your precious contribution as an individual.

It is time to eagerly embrace the development of your positive contribution. Your human personality is realizing the benefit of honoring yourself and being in service. Your soul is eager to complete the long journey from your origin in Oneness through many lifetimes of developing personal wholeness and constructive contributions. This is the soul's *journey of return* leading back to grateful reunion with God.

The cosmos continues to evolve. All growth, all learning, all connection, and all expressions of Love create even more potential for the same. Every one of us is eternal and can be a worthy co-creator with God. The process of living and co-creating is meant to be interesting, productive, and fulfilling in every dimension of existence.

Planet Earth is a school for learning to take personal responsibility as a creator and for learning to discern the truth amid very convincing illusions. Mastering the fundamentals of creating a loving and God-centered process of living, even when circumstances are difficult, is vitally important to your soul's development. Think about what it means to be eternal, to live and evolve forever. Since you are eternal, your highest aspiration as a soul is not arrival at a specific spiritual milestone. Instead, continually improving the never-ending process of elevating your consciousness and service is your most noble goal. Your potential for spiritual growth is ongoing and infinite. You are a precious contributor to Creation.

An essential element of your developmental process is learning to live in the now. Be fully present in each moment so awareness can bring insight. Keep your heart open to accurately sense the truth; be aware of all your feelings because this is the way you receive your guidance from God. You can then choose your attitude and response. These choices are the way you influence the quality of your reality.

Your Divine Guidance comes to you in the moment. Any judgment, denial, numbness, or resistance is quite counterproductive. These defenses tend to close your heart, limiting your perception and obscuring truth. These attitudes delay your personal healing and the blossoming of your co-creative abilities. You are creating right here and now. Be sensitive to the energies and nuances of the present moment.

Time is a feature of *physical* reality. You have

incarnated here to experience the illusion of sequential time. You want to clarify for yourself the relationship between cause and effect because you are learning about how you and others create. Experiencing causes and results separated by an interval of time helps you notice consequences developing and helps you understand your role as a creator. How you choose to respond in any moment affects all the other moments that you and others experience. Since we are all connected, we all have an effect on each other and on the totality of Creation. None of us will be completely successful until we are all successful.

God's Love for us is perfect and everlasting. God is dedicated to supporting each of us in reaching our highest potential. Let us in turn dedicate ourselves to God and to serving the Divine Plan. Let us join together in transmitting sacred Love through our open hearts into every aspect of reality that we experience. The ways Divine Love will be expressed and shared are as varied as the multitude of beings in the universe. Each of us can invent new ways to express the Great Love and to care for Creation.

It is the intentions that we choose to develop within our hearts, along with our actions, that influence the nature of the reality being reflected back to us. Let us create compassionately, fairly, generously, and responsibly. There is a glorious awakening and transformation emerging worldwide, for it is our heart's desire and our destiny to bring this about. Let us create it sooner rather than later!

A similar message of Love is being expressed through many beautiful beings in your cultural and spiritual environments. Divinely inspired Lightworkers functioning as World Servers are found in every society and in every walk of life. Exceptional spiritual volunteers have been present in every era of your history. Some individuals who have made contributions have been aware of receiving Divine inspiration, and some have not. Some have been noticed and respected, while others have not been recognized in your world.

It is your responsibility to use discernment about what to believe. There are reliable ways to determine if an individual or group is truly aligning with Love and wisdom from God. They should not be evaluated by their status in the eyes of men, although communicators of truth are often recognized in this way. They should not be evaluated by their compatibility with the leaders or ideals of their society, for they are often ahead of their time. Your evaluation should be based on considering two things: the example or message itself and the response it generates within you.

Messages of spiritual truth emphasize Love, unity, and communion with God rather than righteousness. Divine Love is compassionate and supportive rather than judgmental. Divine Love is uplifting; it inspires us to be the best we can be as we receive it through many varieties of expression. Divine Love also inspires us to help others be the best they can be.

The second basis for evaluating expressions of truth and Love is the response you feel within your own heart. Let your feelings of attraction or disinterest influence your direction. Explore philosophies, relationships, work, and creative expression that you resonate with, allowing others to do the same. On the other hand, allow yourself to pass by those explorations that do not interest or inspire you.

As you notice your emotions, realize that a strong reaction against something is not the same thing as disinterest. If you are feeling intense emotional upset or rejection of something, recognize that this is an unresolved reaction of your personality. It indicates resistance to an area your soul needs to examine, usually for the purpose of healing, self-forgiveness, or dissolving an illusion of separation.

You may feel an emotional reaction of judgment toward others triggered within yourself when you are clinging to control in order to keep from becoming like them. This is an illusion of separation. You might judge others or their experience because you have blamed yourself in your current lifetime or in a past life for something similar. This is often beyond your conscious awareness.

When an issue has truly been resolved within your heart, you feel an internal acceptance when it comes up. You have tolerance for others and their behavior, choices, or points of view, even if you choose to disagree with them. You do not feel tension or a persistent upsetting reaction unless there is a personal issue coming up for your attention. Instead of being destabilized by your emotional reaction to something that has happened, you can lessen the charge you feel about the situation by coming to full self-responsibility. Take it to God. You may need to seek healing or take action in some area. You can reach a genuine feeling of calm and freedom to make decisions according to your own discernment and internal guidance.

As you move forward in your life, realize that you have the capacity to tap in to Divine inspiration and your own originality. The expression of individual creativity can have many marvelous forms. Your expressive gift is already inside you; it is part of the magnificent radiance of your own Divine nature. Perhaps you are not yet aware of it. You may still need to trust your inner self more in order to become dedicated to your unique Divine expression.

You may have experienced evidence of the gifts within yourself as curiosity, imagination, or a deep longing for what you would love to do in your life "if only." If only you had the time, freedom, money, community of support, education, confidence, opportunity, and so on. You do not need these things in order to begin. Your Higher Self will provide them for you as they become appropriate.

All you need to begin is personal willingness to heal and grow, to ask God for the help you need, and to act in response to your higher guidance. Start with willingness. Dedicate your heart to your partnership with your soul, your Higher Self, and God. Together you can create magic and miracles!

The planetary transformation now underway is leading Earth to a New Age of unprecedented peace and progress. There are specific technological breakthroughs that will not be appropriate for planet Earth until a widespread spiritual evolution takes place. Your spiritual expansion will make it possible to develop certain revolutionary technologies that will improve life for everyone in your world. As technological advancement proceeds, a majority of humanity with sincere spiritual commitment will be necessary to ensure safety for life on planet Earth.

The coming era will be a time of innovation, sharing, and choosing worldwide unity. Many dedicated beings in other dimensions will help to bring it about in response to mankind's seeking and efforts. The aspiration, dedication, and Love must flourish first in individual hearts. Then individuals in physical bodies and beyond will gladly join our various talents together so we can contribute most effectively. We will communicate and cooperate in beautiful loving service to God and to the entire family of life. This process is blessed.

The miracle will happen, dear friend. We will join with you, first in the work and then in the rejoicing. Peace on Earth and goodwill to all! Our hearts are united with yours in Love, in purpose, and in solidarity.

> We bless you.
> Your loving Guides and Friends in spirit
> Amen. Let it be.

Thank you for joining me in this exploration. If you found *Love Letters from Spirit* valuable, you can help to share it with others by posting a review on Amazon or Goodreads.

If you would like to receive my periodic newsletter, Heart and Quill, containing my channeled prayers and additional inspired writing, please visit my website: www.lauradickensonauthor.com.

In Oneness,

Laura

Made in United States
North Haven, CT
31 December 2021